360 D

This is absolutely awesome....I love every minute of it. I don't know what to say so I'll have to put it in a small poem:

"Teachings"

The black soul has reached out to carry the message of life;
The black pain to brush its lips against my forehead and bury itself within my heart;
The black story to couple with my psyche and cause one's healing to commence;
The black woman to pass along the story of reality to her audience – true to form.

Thandisha has walked the pathway of knowledge, love and pain - a book of education to become;
The innate mother to find the strength to shake the demons and rise again with nature's alarm clock;
The woman to wrap herself in the petals of old value while her rocky road cuts at her feet with each step;
The foster supporter of a sibling to reap the blessings of God's mercy through an innocence's forgiveness
The spirit of God within us to shine through the darkness and hold onto our feeble hands - life begins again.

Andreas to shake the foundation of a woman's core and start the achy need for eternal love;
The man to become a king before the eyes of an outside viewer and a love he will never know exists;
The father to make proud many nations of warriors who should respect his actions - the viewer's son will;
The lover to conquer the world and become the richest of most men – a deserving compensation for the struggle;
And faith, love and God's will to rescue this hurt soul and deliver him to a peaceful place of rest - the viewer prays.

The author has performed a gracious and phenomenal action of love for the viewer who transcribes these verses;
The author of Thandisha's & Andreas's life has crossed the seas of charity and oneness - many blessings in sight;
The author's seeds will honor the trials and tribulations of this queen with Africa's rose petals to crown her reign;
And the prayers of long life, love, happiness, mercy and much success will be uttered to God daily for "esta reina".

By Desiree Quildan, Poet

360 Degrees…

Life is a Full Circle

A Novel by Regina Neequaye

*RN*eequaye *P*ublishing
P.O. Box 93851
Atlanta, Georgia 30377

Copyright 2003 by Regina Neequaye
Cover illustrations by Kym Balthazaar
Cover layout by Kym Balthazaar
Visit author's website at www.reginaneequaye.com

ISBN: 0-9718860-3-2

Library of Congress Control Number: 2002090585

Printed in the United States by Morris Publishing
3212 East Highway 30
Kearney, NE 68847
1-800-650-7888

For Zilphia and Jerry Phillips

Rest in Peace

Acknowledgements

I would like to give thanks to my creator who in the midst of a storm made his presence known. I would also like to thank my mother Marjorie Renee Monnigan Reynolds who gave me the gift of compassion. To my three beautiful children: Reynolds, Jordan, and Monnighan. You guys are my inspiration and my reason for being. To my sisters: Denise, Shela, and Vonetta, your support and love is abounding. To cousin and friend, Tina Oda, there are no words to express my sincere gratitude. You were truly there cuz. To Parlee Crowell, Barbara Sanders thanks for the generosity; it was always right on time.

To Lamar Crowell thanks for the beautiful daughters. To Major Callaway thanks for the beautiful son.

To everyone that takes the time to read this work, thank you.

360 Degrees…

Life is a Full Circle

When I pass my sister at high noon and there is not sunlight in her life and she appears bewildered, dazed and half out of her mind. I will not judge her. I will envelope her in a loving, compassionate prayer.

Regina M. Neequaye

0^0
Zero Degrees

I heard a loud, hollow popping followed by an eerie, echoing silence. I slowly walked into my parents' room. Momma was a folded heap in daddy's arms. Blood oozed out of her head slowly dripping down daddy's bare shoulders. Daddy was crying without making sound. The house was so silent that the quietness was more frightening than the morbid vision of my momma and daddy. Tears rolled down his face one at a time. I was numb and in shock. I didn't feel anything. Though I was only 12 years old, I knew I was supposed to be scared, crying or something, but I was numb. I walked down the hall. Khalid stood still in the threshold of his bedroom door. His eyes spoke what his mouth could not. His eyes were blank, looking at me but not actually seeing me. He knew something happened That Day. He knew something happened that would finalize our life the way we knew it. I ordered him back inside of his room. He went back inside of his room, climbed onto the bed, and curled his body tight in a fetal position. I went to his room and closed his door. I walked back into my parents' room, picked up the phone, and dialed 911.

"911 operator."

"My daddy hurt my momma!"

"How did he hurt her?"

"I think he shot her with a gun."

"Honey stay on the line! Help is on the way!" The operator sounded frantic. I thought she was supposed to remain calm and reassure me. Instead, I felt the need to reassure her that I was okay.

"Does your daddy still have the gun?"

"I don't know."

"Is your momm...?"

I placed the phone down and sat next to daddy. I squeezed my head between daddy and momma and sat still. The room was so quiet that I could actually hear our hearts beat.

Blue lights flashed through the curtains. A faint knock echoed through the house. I couldn't move. I wanted to answer the door, but I sat still. I could not move. A loud bang reverberated through the house. I heard an army of footsteps coming down the hall towards momma and daddy's bedroom. There was what seemed like a thousand policemen in full riot gear standing in my parents' room.

"Turn the girl a loose!"

"Let the girl go!"

Daddy didn't move. He appeared oblivious to the small army that occupied the bedroom. He held momma and sat quietly with tears rolling down his face. The police had guns drawn and pointed at daddy's head. I heard a clicking sound and squeezed out of daddy's arms. I was abruptly grabbed and rushed out of the room; the police officer did not wear the standard blue uniform. He was dressed in blue jeans and a sweaty, dingy gray t-shirt. I could feel a gun on my leg, as he held me and ran with me out of the house.

Everything was going so fast. The ambulance's spinning red lights made me dizzy. I thought they were coming to take my mother to the hospital and make her better. I still did not realize she was actually gone until I saw her neatly wrapped in a thick, black, plastic bag. I remember thinking to myself *I wish they would open the bag, so she could breathe.* I wanted to scream. I wanted to shout to momma *here I am please come and get me; I'm over here.* I wanted to cling to her and feel her soft chest close to my face one more time. I wanted to feel her warm arms tightly wrapped around me. I wanted to see her beautiful smile, the smile that was always so reassuring. I knew this was not going to happen ever again.

I don't know how long I stood outside before the police officer brought Khalid to me. The sullen look on his face made me cry. It was a sadness I have never seen on anyone's face before, and I felt a deep, penetrating melancholy. I have never felt this sadness before. We were both crying. He ran to me. He jumped into my arms and tightly wrapped his arms and legs around me burying his face in my neck. He was almost as tall as me; I couldn't believe that my skinny legs were strong enough to hold the both of us. We stood outside for a long time while the policemen were talking to one another, going back and forth, and inside and outside of the house before they took us to the police station.

Grandma was at the police station when we arrived. She was sitting in a dingy, rank smelling room. The walls were made of cinder blocks covered with chipping, gray paint that appeared centuries old. The room was sparsely decorated with a light that hung down from the ceiling over an old, wooden table. Grandma seemed so small sitting at that table. Her eyes were puffy. It seemed as if her whole body was shaking. Khalid immediately ran to her. I stood motionless, unable to move. Grandma came over and gently touched my shoulders. She attempted to pull my rigid body close to her. I put up as much resistance as my thin body would allow.

"Don't worry baby; Grandma will take care of you. I am going to take good care of you." I couldn't respond. It was like I

3

was dreaming; the kind where at the end of the dream you figure out that it's not real, but you still can't awaken and leave the dream. This was not a dream. This was real. I could not awaken and run to my momma and daddy's room and snuggle close between them where even if they didn't wake up, feeling their warm bodies made everything okay.

Grandma's house was no longer familiar to me. My relationship to this house had changed; it was a place where I used to come and visit but then return to my own house. Now I would have to live here. I was no longer going home to my own house to my own things to my momma and daddy.

I was lying in the bed trying not to fall asleep. For the first time in my life, I was afraid. I was afraid, but I didn't know what I was afraid of; it was not an object but a feeling that I couldn't touch. I couldn't describe this feeling. I could not call it a name. There were no words to describe a feeling so sad. This was the first time in my life that when I awakened, I would not know what the day would bring.

Momma was ritual. I knew that every morning she would come into my room and gently touch me. Though I would already be awake, I would not get out of the bed until she came into my room. She would either make oatmeal or French toast if it was a weekday, or she would make a three course breakfast if it was the weekend, but I no longer knew what would happen. I was fearful, and I was hurting. It was an abysmal hurt that ran deep, a continual pain without relief.

I was awakened by the sunlight peeping through the blinds. It took a minute for me to realize I wasn't in my bed. I looked at myself; the bloodstain on my shorts brought me back to the present. I lay back down on the bed and cried. I cried because my momma would never hold me again. She would never part my hair straight when I could not see the back of my head. She would never come in the bathroom and wash my back. She would not see me grow into a woman and see herself in me.

4

I cried because I wanted to be in my own home. I wanted to be in my own room in my own bed. Grandma came into the room. She attempted to touch me. I did not want her to touch me. She tried to hold me. I wiggled out of her arms and ran out of the room.

"Thandisha! Thandisha!" She looked helpless, but I was too absorbed in my own pain to feel her pain. I ran down the hall screaming and crying, "I want my momma." Grandma looked broken. She looked tired and worn. She came closer with her arms spread and her hands open in a come to Jesus stand that Reverend Deal does on Sunday at the end of church service when he invites the congregation to come to Jesus.

"No! Don't touch me Grandma. Don't touch me! I want my momma!" I didn't want to feel anyone's hands but momma's. I didn't want to feel hard, wrinkled hands. I wanted momma's soft, perfect and loving hands to touch me.

"Thandie, baby, your momma is with God. God has called her home." She slowly walked towards me. I walked backwards away from her moving my head from side to side in disbelief at Grandma's words.

"I hate God. Why didn't he call you home? You are old and tired. I want my momma! Where's my daddy? I'm calling him to come and get me out this house!" I walked towards the phone screaming so loud that I could hardly talk. My throat and neck were hurting. I walked to the kitchen, picked up the phone and began to dial. I hoped daddy would answer the phone, come to grandma's house and take me back to my own house with my own things. I wanted to be in my own bed.

"Thandie, remember last night Thandie!" she screamed while snatching the phone away from me. "Your daddy killed your mother! He killed my daughter!" Her words were piercing; they cut deep. They took away my final hope that last night was a dream and That Day really didn't happen.

"You're a goddamned liar Grandma. Don't say that to me. Don't you lie to me Grandma! You're a liar! Where is my daddy?" She slapped me so hard that my neck popped. Her face was tight. It seemed as if every blood vessel in her face was at the surface of her skin.

"Don't you ever mention that man in this house again!" I ran to the kitchen, opened the backdoor, and ran out of the house. I ran hard and fast; Grandma could not keep up. She shouted to Mr. Nance for help. Grandma and Mr. Nance ran after me. I ran. I ran fast. They were behind me. David, Mr. Nance's son, joined them. He was younger than Grandma and Mr. Nance. He caught me and tackled me to the ground. I kicked and screamed. They held me down, and I passed out. When I awakened, I was in bed with Khalid still in Grandma's house.

The funeral was quiet and quick. Aunt Mary wore a black pants suit that was identical to Grandma's suit; the difference was Grandma wore a skirt instead of pants. Khalid wore his favorite black suit with a clip on tie. Daddy tried to teach him to tie a necktie, but Khalid could never get the hang of it. I wore a black dress and black nylons. People I had never seen before came to the front of the church and said nice things about my momma. I held Khalid's hand the entire time. Older women in the church walked by Grandma and firmly placed their hands on her shoulder. I tried to be strong until Aunt Mary touched me. I looked at Aunt Mary; tears began to form in my eyes. I closed my eyes as tight as I could to keep the tears from flowing. I bit my lip in a futile attempt to stop the tears. I could not stop them. They quickly escalated from a slow drip to a full flow.

"Please God bring her back." Aunt Mary gently squeezed my shoulder.

"Aunt Mary, please ask God to bring her back." The church was quiet. The minister stopped speaking and looked at me in a sorrowful, powerless way.

"Baby, the Lord gives, and the Lord takes away."

"No, don't tell me that! I want my momma! Tell God to bring her back, please. I will be so good. I will take communion every first Sunday. I will say my prayers. Tell God I will do anything just bring her back."

No one had answers. The church was dead quiet. Then Mrs. Gigs, an usher that has been at St. James A.M.E., as long as there has been a St. James A.M.E., placed her arms around me and escorted me outside. Aunt Mary followed behind us. I stayed with Aunt Mary while everyone, including Grandma, went to the burial site. I sat on Aunt Mary's lap curling my torso so that I could place my head in her chest. The sound of her heart was a calming lullaby. I wanted to stay there forever until God called me home. After the funeral, we returned to Grandma's house. We did not go to the church for the huge dinner.

Everyone, including Grandma, stayed in their rooms for a week. Khalid and I ate cold cuts, cookies and potato chips the entire week Grandma was in her room. We had not gone to school in almost two weeks. I was not ready to go to school. I could have cared less if I ever saw another school again. Aunt Mary came every morning and stayed late in the evening to take care of Grandma. Khalid and I took care of each other.

"You know guys, we're going to register at your new schools tomorrow."

"Aunt Mary, I am not going to school."

"Sure you are Thandie."

"Oh no I am not. Besides, I don't know anyone at the new school."

"Yeah me neither. I am not going to school either. Am I Thandie?" Khalid repeated everything I said.

"Look guys do you think your mother would want you to behave this way? You know Riley wanted very much for you guys to have a good education." Aunt Mary had a point.

7

Momma taught Khalid and me to read before we went to school, but I really didn't care what Aunt Mary said. I wasn't going to school, and in my mind, no one could make me.

Khalid and I refused to get out of bed and go with Grandma and Aunt Mary to register at our new schools. We were both plagued with a terrible stomachache and blurred vision. We were determined that we were not going to school. I am sure that Aunt Mary and Grandma knew that our sudden illnesses were unreal, but we were allowed to stay home.

When Aunt Mary came back with our room assignments and bus schedules, Khalid and I were speechless. The thought of going to school terrified me. We had grown comfortable staying in the house all day. We had become accustomed to basically doing whatever we wanted. Grandma stayed in bed all day, and we basically had to fend for ourselves. Aunt Mary tried to get us to go outside to play, but we weren't having it. There were a lot of children in the neighborhood. The children appeared friendly, but I really didn't feel up to playing with children. My life was not a child's life anymore; my childhood was stolen in one second with one bullet.

Aunt Mary nagged Khalid and me daily about staying in the house. She constantly reminded us of the need for fresh air. After daily pressure from Aunt Mary, Khalid and I finally went outside the day before we were forced to go to school. There were kids outside playing, but we stayed with each other safe in Grandma's yard.

"Hi I'm Ayanna. What's your name? You want to play Double Dutch?" We were standing outside when Ayanna jumped rope all of the way up the driveway. She looked silly. She had two ponytails, one on each side of her head that flopped up and down every time she jumped the rope.

"No she doesn't want to play with you. Do you Thandie?"

"No," I looked at her and wondered why she wanted to play with a dead woman's child anyway. She had a glow and an aura of innocence that I no longer possessed.

Khalid and I went back in the house, leaving her standing alone in Grandma's yard. I looked out of the window and watched Ayanna play with some of the other neighborhood children. They were playing double dutch, laughing, and talking. I was envious of their happiness and jovial dispositions. I closed the blinds and played card games with Khalid until it was time for bed.

The next morning, Aunt Mary came for Khalid and me to take us to school. When she came in my room and awakened me, I looked at her with a piercing, blank stare.

"Come on Thandie, you and Khalid have to get up. It's time to go." I propped myself on my elbows and continued to stare at her. I thought to myself. *Where in the hell does she think we're going? I told her that I was not going to school.*

"What time is it Aunt Mary?"

"Six o'clock now get up!"

"For what?"

"You are going to school."

"No I am not going to school."

"Oh yes you are. Now get up!" She came over, grabbed my arm and pulled me out of the bed. I tried to grab onto the side of the bed to stop her. She snatched me up and firmly demanded that I get dressed. "Don't upset your brother. You have to go to school and that's all there is to it."

Aunt Mary was right. Khalid would become upset if I were upset. He used my emotions to define his own. If I am happy, he is happy. If I cry, Khalid cries. So I knew if I put on a show, then Khalid would join me.

"Come on Khalid; it's time to get up. You're going to school." She awakened Khalid.

"Thandisha, are we going to school?"

"Yeah, I guess so." I didn't want to upset Khalid. I knew Aunt Mary was serious. We were going to school.

Aunt Mary made oatmeal and toast with a bowl of fresh fruit on the side. We ate breakfast in silence.

"Thandisha, do you need help with your hair?"

"No, I can do it myself." I didn't want anyone's hands to touch me but my momma's.

"Well it's time to leave the table and get dressed, so we won't be late." A wide, genuine smile covered her face; I hoped she was not expecting one in return. I didn't see anything to smile about. I was not ready to go to school and really didn't care if I ever went again. I wanted to stay safely tucked away in my room with my brother forever.

We took Khalid to his new school first. I didn't want to upset him, so I smiled a lot pretending I was okay. I wanted him to know that he would be okay. Actually, if he felt anything close to the way I felt, it's amazing he went inside of the building. Khalid went to his class smiling. After we dropped Khalid off, it was my turn.

"Thandie, you will be okay. I know that it has been hard for you and your brother, but you will be okay." I didn't say anything to her. Right now, she was not exactly my favorite person in the world. I sat staring out of the passenger side window holding my bookbag tightly to my chest.

The building was humongous. It looked as if it would swallow me. I sat in the car with my head turned away from Aunt Mary; I didn't want her to see me cry. I wiped my eyes and opened the car door. I wanted to step out of the car and run, but I knew Aunt Mary could probably catch me. I grabbed my book bag and got out of the car without saying goodbye. I didn't look back when I heard the car door close. I walked in the building and followed the directions to the guidance counselor's office as Aunt Mary instructed. She had already enrolled me, but I had to get my class schedule from the counselor. I have never had to go to school alone on the first day before. Momma always came with me on the first day. She would even walk me to my class on the first day to school.

The guidance counselor gave me a class schedule, a school map, and sent me on my way. I had to find the classes on my own. I walked down the hall looking straight ahead with my belongings held tightly against my chest. I didn't want to see faces, and I didn't want anyone to see my face. I wanted to melt and disappear into the yellow, cinder block, walls. I desperately wanted to become an inanimate object that did not feel, like the round, brown clock that hanged lopsided above the counselor's desk. The halls were crowded. I was scared. I wanted to go in the bathroom and stay until it was time to go home until I saw Ayanna.

"Hey girl," Ayanna acted as if we were the best of friends.

"Hi," I didn't look at her. I continued to walk staring straight ahead with my bookbag still held tightly against my chest.

"Where are you going? What class do you have this period?" She took my schedule from my hand. "Okay let me see. Girl we have English together; come on let's go." She took my arm and dragged me down the hall.

Ayanna and I have been friends since. She has been my anchor to the outside world for the past five years. My grandmother says that we are conjoined twin because we do everything together. In junior high school, we were inseparable. Now in high school we are still best friends. I love Ayanna and Ayanna loves me because I love her. I thanked God for this relationship. She never asked questions about my momma and daddy, but I am sure she knew. The fact that she never asked was an indication she knew.

Ayanna was very popular in high school. I stood in the background. She was a cheerleader; she ran track. I went to the games to see her cheer, and I went to the track to see her run. I went to church to see her sing in the youth choir. Ayanna was the younger of two children. Her life reminded me of what my life would have been, if I still had my parents. She was happy and enjoying her life. I was happy enjoying her life until I met Andreas; I didn't really have a life of my own. My life was Ayanna's life and whatever made her happy made me happy.

When I first met Andreas, I felt like he was an angel sent directly to me from God. He was tall and muscular with perfect, white teeth. He had a fellow classmate by the collar pressed against the wall. There was something about the way he gritted his teeth that caught my attention; they were pearly white, straight and perfect.

"Come on man let me go." The guy was not putting up a great deal of resistance.

"Hell no! If you fuck with my sister again, it's me and you." Drake, a fellow classmate tried to separate them.

"Come on man let him go! You don't need to get in trouble. Your sister gone do what she gone do." Drake managed to pull him away, and they walked down the hall passing my locker. He didn't notice me; I started playing detective. Andreas was the subject of my investigation. I learned that he was a senior; and as fine as he was, he didn't play school sports. He lived on the south side of Atlanta in Zelphie Phillips Homes, one of the toughest government housing neighborhoods in Atlanta. It was rumored that the police wouldn't even go there. Andreas Booker worked after school for one of the factories to help take care of his mother and younger sister, Jazmyne. I dreamed about him day and night, and he didn't even know that I existed. I had already decided when we would marry, the number of bridesmaids, grooms, and the number of little Andreases I would have; and he didn't even know my name or that I occupied a spot on the planet.

Ayanna, who was conducting an investigation of her own, found that he did not have a girlfriend. She invited him to our lunch table. I begged her not to, but she wouldn't listen. "Thandisha, I am tired of your ass asking me about the damn boy; it's time y'all met." She stood and motioned for him to come to our table. I tried to pull her back down to her seat. I grabbed her arm. She quickly snatched away.

"Oh my God, he is coming." Initially, I couldn't talk. He sat down at the table; I noticed his arms were very muscular. He looked like a grown man as opposed to a high school senior.

"Hey I'm Andreas." I was mute. "Ayanna said that you wanted to meet me." I looked down at the table too afraid to look up. Ayanna nudged my side with her elbow.

"Oh yeah I've been seeing you around, and I wanted to meet you." I looked up and was blinded by his pearly whites. I was so mesmerized that I didn't see a complete face but a blurred image. I tried to control my breathing because I felt that I would pass out at any moment.

Before I could continue a conversation, his classmate, Drake, came over.

"Hey man what's up?" Andreas stood and turned around.

"Hey I'll see you around, and what did you say your name was?" I couldn't say anything; I smiled and stared at him until he was out of my view.

"Come on girl let's go before we're late to class." I walked to class with Andreas on my brain. I sat through English, Math, Science, and Social Studies daydreaming about him. I saw him in the senior hall while changing classes for about two months. He would speak to me but that was it. He did not engage in conversation with me or show an interest in me.

I didn't have a conversation with him again until I saw him at Ayanna's backyard pool party. My grandmother was strict; I couldn't wear a swimsuit. I felt awkward as everyone was dressed for the occasion. I wore shorts. He glided over to me. He was wearing black swim shorts. I looked down at his muscular thighs and bulging calves up to his six-pack stomach and then at his pearly whites.

"Hey Thandisha, what's up girl?" I couldn't say anything. All I could do was smile.

"Where is your swimsuit?" He looked down at my legs.

"I'm too skinny to wear a swimsuit in public." I lied; I couldn't very well tell him my grandmother wouldn't allow me to wear one.

"You're small framed, but you're not skinny. You're what I call slim-fine. I bet you look good as hell in a swimsuit." He looked at me from head to toe. I didn't say anything; I couldn't say anything, so I smiled. Then the DJ played my favorite slow jam. I surprised myself by asking him to dance.

"Sure but Thandisha I have never slow danced before." I was shocked; he looked like he had done a lot of things.

"Well I remember hearing someone say you simply sway to the music." We swayed side to side. I placed my arms around his bulging shoulders. His big, hard working hands felt light as a feather on my waist. The song was over, but my face was still buried in his chest. He stepped back away from me.

"You're a good dancer." I was still mute. I simply smiled. I remember this night as if it were yesterday. I felt happy and sad at the same time. I know that sounds oxymoronic. I couldn't explain this feeling. I walked back to the table and sat with Ayanna; he followed me.

"You want something to drink?"

"Sure," he glided to the refreshment table. I didn't take my eyes off of him until he was back at the table.

"Thandisha, you belong to someone?" I didn't know what to say; I simply smiled.

"No she doesn't have a boyfriend." Ayanna intervened just in time.

"That's good." He smiled. It was getting late; I knew I had to be home by 11:00, but I didn't want to leave.

"Girl, it's 10:45; we told your grandmother you would be home before 11:00. Come on let's go; I'll walk you half of the way home." Ayanna was always so responsible. She always stayed out of trouble. I guess that's why Grandma was happy when we became friends. Ayanna was my first and only friend since I lived with my grandmother. Other children in the neighborhood simply stared at me. They were never mean, but it was obvious to me that they knew about That Day. I didn't blame them or become angry with them. I am sure they were afraid to be my friend. Maybe they were afraid my daddy would kill them or their momma. They stayed away and simply didn't talk to me, but not Ayanna. I was mean to her and rebuffed her initial invitation for friendship. But when I saw her on my first day at school, she was exactly what I needed. If it were not for her, I probably would not have made it through the first day.

"Where do you live?"

"Around the corner."

"You want me to walk you home?" I stood, started walking, and he followed me. I was so mesmerized that I didn't tell Ayanna I was leaving. I tried to walk as slowly as I could to savor the moment.

"You live in a nice neighborhood."

"Thanks," Grandma took some of the insurance money and paid off her house. Momma was so smart. She had over $200,000 in life insurance plus a good bit in a savings account. She left Khalid and me $50,000.00 each, but we cannot touch it until we are 20 years old. This would later prove to be a gift to me for a new life, a resurrection.

"You're very pretty Thandisha." When we reached the driveway, I wanted him to kiss me; instead, he gently reached for my hand. "I would like to spend more time with you."

"Thandie! Thandie!" I looked over my shoulder; Grandma was standing in the threshold of the door in her robe and slippers. She didn't have to say anything. I knew she meant for me to come inside of the house.

"Coming Grandma."

"Hello Ma'am." Andreas greeted her. She quickly slammed the door without acknowledging his greeting.

"Thandie?" He smiled torturing me with his beautiful, pearly white teeth.

"That's what my grandmother and brother call me. Actually when my brother was small, he could not say Thandisha, so he would call me Thandie."

"Well Thandie what are you doing tomorrow?"

"I'm not sure. I have to see what Ayanna says, but we will probably go to the mall and catch a movie."

"What time? Would you like for me to give you guys a ride?"

"I would love that, but Grandma doesn't allow me to get into cars with boys." I was waiting for him to say something about the strictness my grandmother imposed, but he didn't.

"If you want to meet us at the mall, we will be there probably around 11:00."

"I'll meet you guys at the Taco Stand say around 12:00." The door opened again. We both looked at one another and smiled.

"Thandie, get in here!"

"Coming."

"Now!" I looked at him. I'll see you tomorrow. I walked up the driveway. Grandma stood at the door waiting for me.

"Who is that boy?"

"Andreas," I walked into the house passing Grandma who was still standing in the threshold of the door. I really didn't want to elaborate on Andreas. I knew she would find something wrong with him.

"How old is he?"

"He is 18 Grandma." I was trying to get away from her. I walked down the hall to my room. She followed me into my room continuing to ask questions.

"He looks like a grown man."

"Grandma, he is18."

"Well where does he live?"

"Down the street."

"I have never seen him in the neighborhood." She was getting on my nerves; I really was not in the mood for twenty questions.

"He works after school Grandma; that's why you never see him. Besides, you never come outside anyway." I knew not to tell her that he lived in the projects; she would go nuts. I walked pass her and went to the bathroom. I turned on the water, so I could get away from her. I was careful not to wash my hands. I wanted to smell the scent of his hands on mine. I looked forward to tomorrow, so I could see him again. I went to bed hoping that I would see him in my dreams.

When I awakened, Khalid was laying at the bottom of my bed. Khalid was 13 years old. He hasn't been able to sleep all night alone since we lived with Grandma. Grandma used to punish him for crying when it was time to go to bed. I made a deal with Khalid when we first moved to Grandma's house; after Grandma went to bed, I would come to his room and get him, so he could go to sleep in my bed with me. I used this to bribe him all of the time; when he wouldn't do as I asked, I would threaten to make him sleep alone in his own bed. The truth of the matter is I needed him close to me probably more than he needed me.

When I opened my eyes again and looked over my shoulder, he was laying behind me with his head propped in his hands.

"Morning."

"Morning." I fell back on the pillow.

"Did you have a good time at the party last night Thandie?"

"Yeah I had a great time. I talked to a really nice guy. I think I'm in love Khalid."

"I'm going to tell Grandma."

"You better not!"

"Thandie, can you take me to the arcade today?"

"No, I am going to the mall with Ayanna."

"There is an arcade in the mall."

"No, I'm not taking you." I got up and pushed him off my bed. He made a loud sound when he hit the floor. I proceeded to make my bed. He got up from the floor with his arms folded across his chest and his eyebrows arched.

"If you don't take me with you, I'm telling Grandma that you're in love with a boy." He knew he had me; and from that moment on, he would bribe me, a trick well learned. I hit him on his shoulder with my fist.

"Grandma, I have something to tell you." He walked towards the door screaming. I grabbed the back of his T-shirt, pulled him back inside of the room, and quickly closed the door.

"You better not tell!"

"I'll be ready in twenty minutes." He stood with his arms folded accross his chest and an annoying smirk covered his face. I was mad as hell. My little brother was now bribing me, and he had me.

Ayanna and I walked down the street to the bus stop; Khalid followed close behind with a victorious smile. He didn't seem to mind that we were totally ignoring him and excluding him from our jokes and laughter.

Although the bus took its usual route, it seemed as if it were taking hours for us to get to the mall. I was anxious. I looked forward to seeing him again. When we finally arrived at the mall, Ayanna and I took Khalid to the arcade. I actually enjoyed the arcade. There were always teenagers at the arcade, but it was something about my little brother, the only person that I could control, now showing power and control that made me nauseous. I didn't even want to play my favorite games.

Ayanna was engulfed in a conversation with Darryl, a boy in our chemistry class. They were playing video games, but I was busy obsessing over my anger at my little brother taking control to join in their conversation. It was 11:30; it seemed as if it took hours for the clock to reach 12:00.

"Come on Ayanna; let's go." She brushed me away. I folded my arms across my chest rolling my eyes; I was mad as hell. I wanted her to leave Darryl and come with me to the Taco Stand. She flipped her hand again, turned her head, and continued to talk to Darryl. I sat on the bench outside of the arcade. It was 12:04. I became increasingly angry and irritated with Ayanna. I walked back inside of the arcade. Ayanna was playing Trooper with Darryl standing close behind her with his arms around her waist.

"Ayanna!"

"What?"

"It's 12:07."

"So?"

"So let's go; you know Andreas is meeting me at the Taco Stand at 12:00."

"He ain't coming here to see me fool; he's coming to see you. You go ahead; I'll stay here with Khalid." It was 12:08. I walked Olympic style to the Taco Stand. I slowly looked around the corner, and I saw him sitting at a table sipping on a soft drink. I quickly slowed my pace. I used my fingers to brush my hair back before I turned the corner. When he saw me, he smiled showing all of his perfect, white teeth. He stood and greeted me, as I reached the table.

"You want something to eat?"

19

"Oh no thank you. I am not hungry." I lied; I hadn't eaten all day. I was too excited; I didn't eat breakfast. I was famished.

"How about a soda?"

"Okay, that would be nice."

"What kind?"

"Strawberry," he walked to the counter and ordered the food. I watched him from the time he left until he returned to the table with four tacos, a taco salad and a burrito.

"Are you going to eat all of that?"

"Girl, this is a snack." He smiled. *God those pearly white teeth.* I laughed. "Here why don't you help me eat?" He unwrapped the burrito and put a small portion inside of my mouth; some of the refried beans fell on the side of my face. He quickly took a napkin and wiped the beans off of my face so gently that I barely felt the napkin touch my skin.

"So what movie are you going to see?"

"I don't know something mild since my little brother came with us."

"You're very pretty Thandisha." He sat still staring at me. I blushed so hard that all 28 teeth were showing.

"Thanks you ain't so bad yourself." The words were coming now. I could actually speak.

"How old is your brother?"

"He is 13, but he will be turning 14 in a couple of days."

"You only have one brother?" He looked surprised.

"Yes I have one brother; it's just me and Khalid."

"What about you?"

"I have four brothers and three sisters. I'm the oldest at home. You know my sister, Jazmyne, don't you?"

"Yes, I have English with her."

"She told me." My heart fluttered. Now I knew he was really interested because he was discussing me with his sister.

"She says that you're very smart and one of the uppity girls."

"I would not say I am uppity." I laughed.

"Hey ain't anything wrong with that. If you got it, you got it. Me, I don't have it, but I am trying like hell to get it. I work the second shift full-time, Monday through Friday. I'm trying to get my own business."

"Really!" I tried to sound interested.

"Hell yeah. You don't make money working for the man. The man gets rich, and you still struggle."

"What kind of business do you want?"

"A lawn service. Oh it is more than cutting grass. See I'm taking horticulture at school. I have four commercial clients already. I'm trying to save up for a riding lawn mower, so I can get some big accounts. I want a zipper. Have you ever seen one?" He was so excited that he didn't allow time for an answer. "Well they go about 50 mph. You can cut a football field in about an hour. That's what I am saving for." He sat back in his chair with his head cradled in his hands.

"So what do you want to do when you graduate?"

"I want to be an artist. Grandma says that it is a waste of time. She says that I'm going to college."

"So you can draw?"

"Oh yeah. I drew all of the art in our house. I've even sold paintings to members of our bible class."

"I'm not saying anything against your grandmother, but I don't see anything wrong with wanting to be an artist if you have the talent."

"Really?" I smiled. No one showed genuine interest when I spoke of my goals not even Ayanna. Though I tell her I want to be an artist, she brushes it off. She has already made plans for us to be college roommates and pledge the same sorority. She hasn't decided on which sorority she wants us to pledge; she says that she will decide when we get to college.

"Hey look at Cynthia St. James, Charles Bibbs those are some pretty cool artists. My favorite is Paul Goodnight." He actually knew about art. I was impressed.

"I love DT Turman."

"I never heard of him."

"Grandma bought me one of his original paintings for my 15th birthday. He's great. He uses raised oil paint mixed with fine granules of sand splattered on canvas."

"Wow I'd love to see it." For some reason, I didn't picture him being the kind who enjoyed art. Though he had a gentle spirit, he looked hard. I think it's his eyes. They looked old and kind of weary as if they had seen a lot of pain and disappointment.

"Hey girl."

"What's up?" It was Jazmyne, his sister. "Give me some money Bro; hell I need to get my damn nails done." She was dressed in a loud orange, tight fitting jumpsuit, loud orange matching shoes, and big gold hoop earrings. Grandma would have called her a ghetto hoochie.

"I told you to stop putting that fake shit on your nails."

"Niggah, just give me the damn money." She propped herself on one leg. He gave her twenty dollars; she smiled showing three gold teeth in the front of her mouth. Her gold teeth looked odd and off centered. I have seen people with one gold tooth. I have also seen them with two, but I have never seen three. I stared into her mouth as she talked trying to figure out the pattern, but I realized there was no pattern.

"Here now go; you need to tell Keekee to get a damn job." She sucked her teeth, rolled her eyes and walked away.

"Damn that girl drives me crazy. This boyfriend that boyfriend and that damn Keekee; I don't even want to go there." He looked up at the ceiling and shook his head. "How many boyfriends do you have?"

"I have never had a boyfriend."

"Baby, you don't have to play me like that. You are way too fine not to have a boyfriend."

"Seriously I've never had a boyfriend." I didn't understand why he found that so surprising. I mean I was not ugly, but no one ever talked to me except for Ayanna. I always figured that people were too afraid to talk to me because of That Day.

"That's hard to believe, but you don't look like a liar to me."

"I need to check on my brother." I looked at my watch it was 1:33. We both stood at the same time. I waited for him while he cleaned the table. He gently placed his hand on the middle of my back and escorted me through the maze of tables and out of the food court.

Ayanna was sitting in front of the arcade on the bench with Darryl.

"Where is Khalid?"

"He is still in the arcade winning tickets trying to get a prize." I walked into the arcade; he followed me. Khalid was playing a video games with a long line of tickets flowing from the machine.

"Khalid!"

"Yeah?" He never looked up.

"Come on it's time to go."

"I'm not ready."

"I don't care. Let's go." I looked down at the tickets running out of the machine and then saw another bag full of tickets next to him.

"Boy, did you spend all of your money?"

"Not yet."

"How much did you spend?"

"Thandie, will you leave me alone?" I snatched him away from the game. He jerked away from me. When he touched the button again, the game ended.

"Thandie, look what you did!" He sat on the floor and rolled all of his tickets into a doughnut shaped circle smiling from ear to ear as if he had found gold. He turned, looked at me, and then looked at Andreas. He didn't say anything to Andreas; he looked at him with a long stare.

"Hey little man what's up?" Khalid took his tickets and walked away.

"Khalid, come here!"

He continued to walk as if he did not hear me. "Now!" He slowly walked over to me.

"What?"

"Let's go and get something to eat. I know you're hungry."

"I want to play some more; I'm not hungry." Andreas reached into his pocket and pulled out five dollars.

"No thank you," he looked at the money and walked back to his game and inserted more coins into the machine.

"Khalid, I'll be sitting on the bench in front of the arcade entrance. When you finish, come out here." We sat on a bench, across from Ayanna and Darryl and talked. He told me his story and shared his dreams. I listened; at the time, I wasn't able to tell him mine. I hadn't dealt with my story yet. I still had nightmares about That Day. I made a conscious decision not to deal with it, not to think about That Day. I rationalized that if I didn't think about it, then the memory would no longer hurt me. I didn't realize that tucking the memories away, deep inside of me, without dealing with them almost cost me my life. It is only now that I know that life is 360 degrees, a full circle. You have to complete the circle. There is no escape. There is no diversion from feeling the pain. The pain cannot lay tucked away forever. The memory will resurface, sometimes at the most inopportune time, and if you don't have the tenacity to deal with them, they could kill you. Not quick, but slow and painful. You have to look at them veraciously, and if you don't, you will have to go back 360 degrees until you face them and face them truthfully.

"Andreas is such a unique name. I have never heard of a black person with that name."

"It came from my daddy. He's the best gambler in the world." He smiled as if this were an admirable trait.

"Are you like your daddy?" His smile quickly disappeared.

"I don't really know because I try like hell to be the opposite. I work hard. I help take care of my mother and younger sister, and I don't have a bunch of baby mommas. I figure my dad has to be pretty sick. He says he loves women, but I don't see it. I figure if you really like women, you would want to savor one particular woman. You love everything about one particular woman. Besides, you all are too complex to deal with more than one at a time."

"What do you mean by complex?" I laughed, but I was annoyed.

"I have three sisters and a mother. Women are something to deal with. Once you think you know what it takes to satisfy a woman, she changes to something else. Women are very hard to please." He looked at me. "Are you hard to please?"

No one ever asked me anything. So I really didn't know how to answer this question. All of my decisions were made for me, or people made decisions and didn't care how they affected me.

"I don't know. No one ever told me that I was hard to please; no one ever said that I wasn't."

"Thandie, I'm hungry." Khalid walked behind the bench and tapped me on the shoulder.

"Okay wait a minute." He waited all of three seconds.

"Thandie, I'm thirsty." I looked over Andreas' shoulder. His arm was around me. Khalid walked in front of the bench.

"Get your hands off of my sister!" He gave Andreas a mean, nasty look.

"Okay little man. I'm sorry; I didn't mean no disrespect." Andreas moved his arm.

"Let's go Thandie!"

"Sit down Khalid, or I will never take you to the arcade again!" He sat down on the bench next to me pouting. I tried to ignore him. I was embarrassed. Khalid is 14, but he is very immature. I know other 14 year olds that are much more independent. I have always tried to be very patient with him. I believe that he regressed about five years after That Day. There are times when he acts his age, but at other times, I swear he acts as if he is nine or ten years old.

"Hey little man, do you want me to walk down to the Taco stand with you? Do you like tacos?" Khalid's demeanor suddenly changed; a big smile covered his face.

"Give me some money Thandie." I reached in my pocket and gave Khalid five dollars. When they returned, Darryl was gone, and Ayanna and I were sitting on the bench in front of the arcade.

"Girl it is 3:00; we missed the movies."

"Yeah I know; we better get ready to catch the bus."

"I can take you home."

"We don't have to be home until 6:30." I told Grandma that I was going to the movies. If we came back too early, she would know I lied.

"We can go to the park, and then I'll drop you guys off at your bus stop." This was a good idea; we still had time to hang out before Grandma expected us home. Besides, I really wanted to spend more time with Andreas.

"We walked to the end of the parking lot to his car. He drove a candy apple red, 67 Thunderbird. It didn't have dents or scratches, and it was clean inside and out. He walked to the passenger side of the car and opened the door for me. I had never ridden in a car with a boy. I felt grown up and mature. I reached over the seat and unlocked the door for Khalid and Ayanna.

"Put your seat belt on Khalid." He rolled his eyes and fastened his seat belt. He used to do everything I told him to do without rebuttal, but now he is beginning to challenge me.

We drove by his home in Zelphie Phillips Downs. His grandmother's apartment was two buildings over from his, and a cousin stayed two doors down from the grandmother. There was what looked like a thousand children playing outside. Women, young and old, were sitting on their porches, and a couple of men with worn faces stood bent over looking under the hood of a rusty old car that appeared too old to consider repairing. There were a lot of people that lived in his apartment complex. I had never seen so many people in one place before.

We drove onto highway 85 then on highway 20; I could see the outline of the park from the freeway. It was beautiful from this view. The trees were green. From this angle, the litter blended in well with the landscape. The abuse of the park was undetectable until you got up close. Then you could see the park's vulnerabilities. The remnants of paper bags half filled with food were obviously litter and not part of the landscape. A faint scent of urine permeated the air. I really don't understand how people could abuse something so naturally beautiful. There were trashcans all over the park, yet the landscape was filled with litter.

Truthfully, I was really never interested in visiting the park, but I enjoyed this time with Andreas. We found an old, oak tree that generously provided shade from the sun. We parked under the tree and listened to reggae music. Reggae really wasn't my thing, but I was enjoying Andreas' company.

Khalid had fallen asleep; we left him in the car. Ayanna found some friends and left Andreas and I alone. We sat on a picnic table next to the car. I sat next to him and stared strait into

27

his eyes. He kissed me without warning. It felt good. His lips were soft and damp but not too wet. I had never kissed a boy before and was surprised at how natural this was for me.

"I've wanted to do that all day." He smiled while licking his lips. I could have stayed with him all day. He was fun and kind. He wasn't hard and callous. He was easy to talk to and very considerate. His conversation was not the kind of conversation I was accustomed to. He was totally different than anyone I have ever known.

I was having fun, but I had to get home before it was too late. I saw Ayanna and yelled for her to come back to the car. We buckled our seat belts and headed home. His eyes were fixated on me the entire trip. I was glad he was a good driver because as often as he glanced at me, he didn't drive off the road. He dropped us off at the corner at 6:45; we were late. I coached Khalid on what to tell Grandma. *The movie was good and scary. We went to see Dinosaur Horror. It was about big scary dinosaurs. It was so scary; I can't talk about it.* When we reached the driveway, I reminded him one more time what to say to Grandma.

"If she asks anything else what are you going to say?"

"Grandma it was so scary; I don't want to talk about it."

"Okay that's good." When we got home, Grandma had already made dinner. I am normally the cook. Grandma never seasoned her food. Her food was always bland. Grandma cooks out of obligation. You cannot taste the love in her food. She made fried chicken, rice, and broccoli. The chicken tasted like chicken and flour. The rice was crunchy and needed more time to cook. The broccoli was plain, no butter or cheese. I hated her cooking because it made me miss my momma. Momma enjoyed cooking. You could taste the love in momma's food. She always took her time and seasoned the food perfectly. The table was quiet as usual. We never really talked to each other, and when we did, it was never about anything meaningful. Our conversations were always superficial.

After dinner, I washed dishes, took a shower, and went to my room. I watched television and waited by the phone praying that Andreas would call me. I sat on the bed and looked in the mirror often glancing at the phone just in case he called. I was a mixture of momma and daddy. My skin was paper bag brown like daddy. My hair was jet black and thick as a rope like momma. I was so glad when Grandma finally allowed me to chemically straighten my hair. Now if I could only convince her to allow me to cut it. It didn't have a style. I always wore it in a bun in the back of my head. I put a rubber band in my hair to make a ponytail then twisted the ends into a bun. Grandma once said that when I took my hair down, I looked like momma. After she said this, I did not wear my hair loose again for years.

"Oh my God Thandisha, you are waiting by the phone." I picked up the phone on the first ring. It was Ayanna. I could hear the television show Grandma was watching in the den. I hated when she listened to my conversation before she hanged up.

"Grandma, I have it." She knew the phone was for me. The only person she ever talked to on the phone was Aunt Mary. And that was not often because Aunt Mary was usually here.

"Hey girl today was so much fun."

"Yeah Ayanna I had a ball girl."

"That Darryl is a trip with his fine self."

"He ain't fine as Andreas."

"Child please, Andreas is not that fine; he's too black."

"What do you mean too black?" Ayanna's phone clicked.

"Girl, that's Devontae. Ooh I love him."

"I thought you loved Darryl."

"I do."

"Well you can't love both of them."

"Why not? I am not trying to marry nobody. Girl we are in high school. We're supposed to have fun." My phone beeped. It was Andreas. I didn't click back over to tell Ayanna that I would call her back.

"Hello."

"Hello, may I speak to Thandisha?"

"This is she."

"Hey, what's up? His voice was low and deep, yet soothing.

"Nothing I am just sitting in my room watching television."

"I was waiting on you to call me. I decided maybe you wouldn't call, so I called you. Were you busy?"

"No, I told you; I was watching television. I was waiting, kind of hoping you would call." He laughed.

"I really had a nice time today. I really dig you girl."

"I kind of like you too." We talked on the phone for over an hour when my line beeped. It was Ayanna.

"Girl, I was sitting and waiting to see how long it would take you to call me back. You know you are through." She laughed, but I could tell she was annoyed.

"I'm sorry Ayanna. I'll call you back in 20 minutes." Twenty minutes turned into an hour. I could not get enough of Andreas.

45⁰

Forty-Five Degrees

Everything in my life has changed. In fact, it is hard for me to remember when my life was not like this. I feel as if I have been an orphan forever. My other life is buried deep inside of my memory, and I can't touch it. I can't go back that far to reach it. This new life was odd and peculiar. I felt as if I would wake up at any moment and find that I have been dreaming. My life didn't feel real. It is as if I were looking in a mirror or an audience member in a theatrical play watching the different characters in my life perform. I have no friends in my life from before That Day. Perhaps if I did, they could remind me who I used to be. I have totally forgotten. I have not gone back to my old house since That Day. I don't know what became of that house.

I found a way to survive in this new life. With the exception of my relationship with my brother, all of my relationships were superficial. It didn't matter because I needed the people in my life to keep me anchored in order to keep my sanity. Ayanna was my superficial best friend. She was happy with our friendship because she was the center of my attention. Living Ayanna's life was appealing to me because I didn't have to live my own life. I didn't have to think about That Day or myself. I don't think I would have survived if I didn't have

Ayanna; she was the center of my attention. Actually, she was the center of everyone's attention including her own.

She was definitely the center of Mr. Williams' attention even at the expense of her older sister, Dee. Ayanna's father gave her a lot of extras. She had the best of everything. Clothes, jewelry you name it; Ayanna had it. She says that it is one of the perks in being the baby of the family. Her parents were still together. Her oldest sister, Dee, and her two children moved back home after a nasty divorce. I am sure Dee felt like a failure. Ayanna had a way of making all of Dee's faults known. In spite of her self-centered nature, I loved Ayanna. I knew her significance to my life.

I enjoyed visiting Ayanna's house. Her home felt peaceful. I believed if That Day had not happened, my family would have been like Ayanna's family. Ayanna was very close to her father. She was a straight A student. Her primary goal in life was to make her daddy proud. Their relationship was beautiful to me. It was as if he were a king and she his princess. When her father would drive us around to the many events that Ayanna was involved in, he would always open the door for Ayanna to get in the car and open the door for her to get out of the car. Ayanna did not consider this treatment special or out of the ordinary. She expected it.

Ayanna's mother was like a shadow. Not only was she in the background in Ayanna's life, but she was in the background of Mr. Williams' life as well. Ayanna rarely spoke of her mother. I thought this shameful. She obviously didn't understand the special nature of a mother. I prayed that she would never feel my loss. I enjoyed sitting in the kitchen talking to Mrs. Williams. It wasn't often that I spoke to her. Ayanna would always want to go into her room when Mrs. Williams came into the kitchen, our normal hang out. She acted as if she didn't want me speaking with her mother like she was ashamed of her mother. I didn't like the way she spoke to her mother. It

32

was as if Ayanna was the mother, and Mrs. Williams was the child. The sad thing about their relationship is that Mrs. Williams appeared to accept it. I don't remember my mother being as docile as Mrs. Williams, but her soft nature was very appealing to me. She was inviting and kind, and I often wanted to run to her and wrap my arms around her skinny, frail body. I never did it though, but I always wanted to embrace Mrs. Williams, and I would sometimes imagine what it would feel like for her to hold me close with her arms tightly wrapped around me.

Grandma always said that women made the best friends. Though our relationship was superficial and centered on Ayanna, she was my best friend, and I loved her. Not the way Grandma loved Aunt Mary. Grandma never told us that she and Aunt Mary loved each other the way a man and a woman love each other, but we knew. Aunt Mary and Grandma have loved each other for years even before I was born. Their relationship began shortly after my mother was born. I never met my grandfather. Grandma never spoke of him. I have a picture of him with momma when momma was little girl. But I never saw him face to face. I have never seen Grandma love a man.

Aunt Mary never spent the night. I never saw them touch, but I knew. It was the way they looked at each other. Aunt Mary was kind of manly not because of her hair. Grandma wore a short natural too, but it was how she did every thing. Grandma was tall and slim like momma and me. Aunt Mary was just as tall as Grandma, but she was heavier. She always wore jeans and male shirts. Aunt Mary never carried a purse. She carried a man's wallet that fit snug in her back pocket.

Grandma was more feminine. She carried a purse, and unlike Aunt Mary, she walked soft and graceful. She was very meticulous about her appearance. Aunt Mary and Grandma's relationship was beautiful to me. They were lovers and best friends. They were very respectful of one another differences as well as their commonalities. Grandma didn't seem quite as comfortable with their relationship as Aunt Mary. Maybe it was because Khalid and I were now living with her. I think Aunt Mary has been a lesbian forever. She was probably born this way, as there was not a feminine bone in her body. In fact, she is often mistaken as a man.

Though Grandma was my blood relative, I felt more comfortable talking to Aunt Mary. She made me feel that I was okay. She harnessed all of my talents. She loved me and loved my art. She framed all of my paintings. Aunt Mary made me feel that it was okay I didn't want to go to college. Grandma planned for me to attend college after I graduated from high school. I think it was because she wanted me out of the house.

Grandma and Khalid got along great. But Grandma and I were always guarded with one another. She never said anything mean. She was not unkind, but it took a lot of effort for us to communicate. I enjoyed doing special things for Aunt Mary because she always noticed the most latent things in me. She discovered my gift for cooking; and because of this, I always enjoyed making special desserts for her. I made pastries, cheesecakes and any kind of dessert they made in the bakery. She would always brag on my cooking. When members of our bible class commented on her weight gain, she would always blame me. Sometimes bible class members would place orders for my sweets and pay me to make them.

Once a week, Aunt Mary would order a cake or pastries for someone on her job. Aunt Mary always said that I was a natural artist, but Grandma was determined I was going to college. I could have gone to college. My grades were good, but I wanted to go to culinary school to master the art of cooking, and I was determined that I would be an artist. I painted beautiful, quality art. I never entered competitions, but I knew that my art was prize winning because it came from my soul.

Sometimes I felt as if Grandma was jealous of my relationship with Aunt Mary. Aunt Mary didn't have expectations of me. She never pressured me to be anything or anyone that I didn't want to be. Our only disagreement was my choice of Ayanna as a best friend. Aunt Mary acted as if she hated Ayanna. She complained that Ayanna bossed me around too much. She always referred to Ayanna as "the Bitch." Grandma loved Ayanna because she was Grandma's idea of what a girl should be. She always commented on Ayanna's stylish clothes and modern hairstyles. Aunt Mary would become angry with Grandma when she made comparisons between Ayanna and I, as she often did. She wanted me to have Ayanna's outgoing personality and her confident disposition, but I didn't have those qualities. Maybe I used to, but I don't have them anymore.

I didn't feel Grandma's love. I knew that she loved me. She had to; I was her only daughter's daughter. But I felt that she hated me for being my daddy's daughter. Although I cannot remember a lot of detail, I do remember a strong feeling for daddy. We were very close. I remember that I was labeled a daddy's girl, and I remember every Friday he would bring Khalid and me presents.

Initially, I tried to please Grandma. I tried to make sure the house was always clean. I was extra careful to season the food properly when I cooked. No matter what I did, it was never good enough; whereas, Aunt Mary was simply cool about everything. I loved Grandma in spite of how she made me feel. I loved her because we shared the same grief. I loved her because her daughter was my mother. Momma was her only child, and I knew she was still in pain. Sometimes at night I could still hear her crying, especially on June 9, momma's birthday, but we never talked about That Day. Everyone came to their own conclusions and made their own reality.

I often worried about Khalid. He had no male role model. I had been hearing people talk about black boys needing good male role models and became concerned. This is one of the reasons I was glad I met Andreas. Aunt Mary was masculine, and she could shoot a basketball as good as any man. Aunt Mary wasn't a man, but she was the closest thing to a male role model that Khalid had until I met Andreas.

Andreas was definitely something good in my life. He made me feel good. I began to feel alive again. He wasn't pushy. I enjoyed talking to him. Unlike most of my relationships with people, my relationship with him was real from the start. I was very comfortable with him. Although he did most of the talking, he was not self-centered. He often asked questions about me. He was genuinely concerned about my thoughts and feelings. Although I rarely had much to say, he at least asked me questions. Unlike Ayanna, he didn't give me the answers to the questions he asked.

Andreas and I were diametrical. Unlike me, he was centered. He knew what he wanted. I came from a background of excess; Khalid and I had every material thing we wanted. With all of the material things I had, I was not anchored. Andreas' family was poor. He works a full-time job to help support his momma and younger sister and still attends school daily. Andreas described a life full of needs, but he was happy, confident, and he knew what he wanted to do with his life.

His mother, unlike Grandma, was nice and pleasant. She always answered the phone with a kind voice. His sister, Jazmyne, was a different story. It's hard to believe they are related. Andreas is calm and subtle. Jazmyne is loud like an explosion. Not only did she talk loud, her whole demeanor was very attention getting. She was always over accentuated. Instead of one nose ring, she had two, one in each nostril. She had a gold stud earring in her chin and a silver stud in her tongue. It was bad enough that she wore those awful crochet braids, but her braids were colorful and moved like a mop with the slightest movement of her head. I am not against braids. Actually, I like braids, but the crochet braids are cheap and tacky. I am not trying to put Jazmyne down; we were actually quite similar. Like me, Jazmyne was deprived of something that she strongly felt she needed. Unlike me, Jazmyne screamed loud for what she needed. Andreas was very protective of Jazmyne. He was willing to throw a punch at anyone he considered a threat to her. He loves Jazmyne the way I love Khalid. Andreas attempted to be a father figure to Jazmyne just as I was trying to mother Khalid. I know it's crazy, but sometimes I found myself jealous of Jazmyne's relationship with Andreas.

90°
Ninety Degrees

The summer was excruciatingly hot. I still don't understand how people live without central air. Before meeting Andreas, I spent my summers in the house until sun down, which was usually around 7:00 p.m. The only time I left the house was to visit Ayanna. If her daddy was in his energy conservation mode, I would go home where it was always cold. But this summer was different. I was in love, and I tried to get out of the house every chance I could. Grandma was never concerned about my whereabouts as long as I was with Ayanna. So when I asked to go to Phillips High School's graduation with Ayanna, she agreed without her usual twenty questions.

I was happy to see Andreas graduate. He went to a special graduation because he was on a technical path diploma. He graduated from our school too, but he was not in the college bound class, which is what Emaline Bowen High School was notorious for. The school produced more college bound students than any school in the county. The legislators in Andreas' district were concerned because some of the tax dollars from their districts were transferred to our school. So the school had to open its doors to a more economically diverse group of students, which is how the kids in Andreas' neighborhood were able to attend. Emaline Bowen High School didn't have a technical tract, so the students that were on a technical tract attended Phillips High School for their specialized technical classes.

He was handsome in his red gown. I had to agree with Grandma; he did look more mature than the other graduates. Normally, she would not allow me to visit this part of town. She always felt that inner city Atlanta was too dangerous. Actually, I did not find it any more dangerous than any other part of the city especially since they were now building new buildings throughout the city and renovating the old ones. Actually, they were moving the poor people out of the city and replacing them with an upper middle class to upper class income population. Even the solidly middle class could not afford to live within the city limit.

Grandma had a class-conscious ideology. She rationalized that as long as the homes were pretty, the lawns well manicured, and the cars in the driveways were up to date models, the neighborhood was nice. It didn't matter what went on inside of the house or whether or not the people in the house were of good character.

Phillips High School did have a reputation. It was the first school to have armed policemen patrolling the hall, which was strange because Phillips High School never had an instance of gun violence at school. Yes, there were a lot of fights but nothing as extreme as what happened at Shelly G. Reynolds High School last year when a rich white kid shot at everyone in the gymnasium during a Physical Education Class. Everyone knew the reason the police patrolled Phillips High School is that the population is one hundred percent black.

After Andreas graduated, we spent time together almost every day before he went to work. I was an upcoming senior, so Grandma reluctantly allowed me more freedom. I am sure she knew she had no choice, but it drove her crazy. I thought we would be talking about safe sex and birth control the way Ayanna's parents did. Ayanna's father made her mother take her to the teen clinic and gave her the choice of getting birth control pills just in case. Instead, Grandma was nagging the hell out of me about college.

"You're spending too much time with that boy Thandie. How are you going to study for the SAT if you are always with that boy?"

"Grandma, he is nice. You don't have to worry; I'm okay." I hated having these conversations with her because no matter what I said she would not be convinced that Andreas was nice and harmless to me. She only allowed him to come inside of the house twice since we've been dating.

"Where did you say he lives again?"

"Around the corner," I hated lying to her, but I didn't want more stress from her about Andreas. If I told her he lived in the projects, she would have a fit. It's not that she thinks she is superior to anyone else, but she is proud of the fact she raised my mother without child support or government assistance. She would always say that she qualified for assistance, and then she would become angry and say that no white man was going to dictate the quality of life that she could give her child. Grandma felt that people should, "work as long as they had two arms, two legs, and half of a back."

"Why don't you go over to his house and meet his parents?" I prayed she would never call my bluff; I knew asking her to meet Andreas' parents was a good way to make her leave me alone. She turned away and washed the same clean glass three times.

"I don't want or need to meet his parents."

"Why not?" The sick thing about this game I played with Grandma is that I didn't want her to meet his parents, but I was mad because she said that she didn't want to meet his parents.

"I don't want to because I don't want to." She dropped the glass, and it shattered all over the floor. She reached down and picked the broken glass off of the floor. I continued to clean the table.

"Grandma, I'm going to Ayanna's house. I'll be back before it's too late." I walked out of the door and was half of the way down the street when I saw the red thunderbird. It was Saturday 12:00 noon; Andreas didn't have to work.

"Hey girl, who you belong too?" He drove the car close to me.

"No one."

"You think I can get them papers?"

"I don't know; it all depends."

"On what?"

"Do you think you can love me forever plus five years?"

"Forever is a long time. He laughed showing his beautiful, white teeth. Come on baby get in the car." I slid in the car leaning over to kiss him before fastening my seat belt.

"What do you want to do today?"

"I don't know." Actually being with him was good enough.

"Hell it's too hot to drive around. You want to get a room?"

"Yeah that's cool." Andreas and I had not had real sex; I sometimes lay on my back, and he gets on top of me and grinds his manhood against me until he climaxes. I never worried about getting pregnant; we kept on our underwear. Most of the time we would rent a hotel room to be alone. I didn't feel comfortable with him coming to my house, and there were too many people who came in and out of his. Today felt different. I was relaxed and very much at ease. We were lying on the bed drinking sodas and eating hamburgers.

"Thandisha, do you remember the first time we went on that pseudo date at the mall?"

"Yeah."

"I asked if you were hungry, and you said no."

"Yeah and so what?"

"Why you lie? I heard your stomach growling loud as hell." I punched him in his chest to stop his laughter. He playfully grabbed me and pulled me close.

"Girl, I sure do love you."

"I love you too." He kissed me strongly and passionately while rubbing between my thighs. I used to lie still, but I found myself opening my thighs and moving my hips with the rhythms of his hand. He pulled my panties off and pulled my dress over my head. I didn't have on a bra; the straps on my sundress were too skinny. He pulled down his shorts and underwear at the same time. We were both naked. He sat upright on the bed and looked down at me with a blank stare.

"You have a beautiful body Thandisha." I looked at his massive chest and six pack stomach. My eyes stopped; I didn't want to look further. He leaned over to the nightstand and pulled a condom from his wallet. He sat on the edge of the bed with his back to me and slipped it on. He rolled back on the bed and covered my body with kisses while gently massaging between my thighs. I jerked in pain when he inserted his finger inside of me. He kissed my forehead and then my mouth.

"It's okay baby. I'm going to be so gentle with you. I'm going to love you forever plus five years." His kisses were soft and gentle. I looked down, saw his erect penis, and sat straight up in the bed.

"Oh my God! Is all of that going inside of me?" He smiled and continued to kiss me. I cried out in pain, as he slowly pushed his manhood inside of me. My body was wreathing in pain, but I loved him so much; I wanted to give him all of me.

"Bite my shoulder baby; hold on to me." I sank my teeth deep into his shoulder. Every time he moved, I screamed.

Finally, he was inside of me. He moaned while slowly moving his hips. I couldn't move. I was too afraid of breaking something. He moaned, made a funny face, and tightened his eyes before collapsing on top of me. He lay still in silence holding me close, kissing my face, forehead, and lips.

"I love you Thandisha."

"I love you too." I rolled over laying my head on his chest and fell asleep...

"Thandisha! Thandisha!" I awakened with him shaking me. "Wake up baby." I awakened crying; he pulled me close wrapping his legs around my entire body. "It's okay baby whatever it is; it's okay. I'm here." I cried for so long that I became light headed. It was 5:30. I knew I should be getting home, but I didn't want to leave. I felt alive. I wanted to talk about That Day, but the words wouldn't or couldn't come. They were lost in a five-year psychosis that allowed me to exist without feeling. They were hidden somewhere deep inside of me, and I couldn't find them. He kept probing me for answers, but I couldn't tell him. I didn't know where to start if I could tell him. We sat still and held one another tightly.

"Thandisha, it's getting late. I'd better get you home." He was right. I was probably already in trouble and should get up and go home.

"I'm not ready to go. I want to stay right here with you."

"Okay baby get dressed; I want to show you something anyway before I take you home." We washed up, put on our clothes, and went to the car. We drove to the West End, a very cultural part of Atlanta filled with African American owned shops, restaurants and sturdy antebellum homes. We drove past Abernathy and then turned onto Mayflower Avenue.

"What do you think?"

"Of what?"

"This is it; this is my apartment." We got out of the car and went up the stairs to a studio apartment. The apartment was spacious with hardwood floors, big windows and a small kitchen. The bathroom was small, equipped with only a shower and toilet.

"I paid for it this morning. I can't get the lights turned on until tomorrow. My sister has to get her bill out of my name."

"It's beautiful Andreas."

"Can I hire you to decorate it?"

"You don't have to hire me."

"You're an artist; you should be paid for your work."

"Please I can draw, and I can cook. I am not an interior decorator." He took a second key off of the key ring and placed it in my hand.

"I don't have to work tomorrow. You think I could get you to come and help me?"

"Yeah, how much do you want to spend?"

"Well it's just me, so I don't need to spend but a grand or so."

"You have a thousand dollars?" I was shocked; a thousand dollars seemed like a lot of money to have at one time.

"I have been working full-time for two years. I should have some money." He locked the apartment door, and we went back to the car.

As usual, Andreas let me out of the car down the street, and I walked to the house. Grandma opened the door before I could place my key in the keyhole. She grabbed a handful of my hair and pulled me into the house. She slapped me so hard that my ears rang. Khalid stood still covering his face.

"Where were you?"

"I was with Andreas." I knew not to add fuel to the fire and lie. She still had a hand full of my hair dragging me down the hall to my room cursing me at the same time, so she obviously knew I was not with Ayanna.

"Damn you Thandisha, you told me you were going to Ayanna's house."

"I changed my mind." I wanted to do some cursing of my own, but I couldn't say anything; she had me. I did lie.

"How many times have you lied to me?" I could see the hurt on her face, but there was nothing that I could do to remove it. I knew she was afraid for me. She had already lost a child, her only child; she didn't want to loose another one.

"You will not see that boy again!"

"What are you saying Grandma? I will see him again!"

"You will not! That boy is bad news! He is a bad influence!"

"I love him, and I will see him again!" I surprised myself by screaming to the top of my lungs.

"Don't you talk to me like that young lady! I have the final word, and you will not see him again!"

"You don't talk to me Grandma; I am just here. You haven't had one honest conversation with me since I have been here. I love him. He talks to me. He cares about what I think. He loves me."

"Shut up girl! You better not say another word!"

"Stop it Thandie stop!" Khalid ran to me. I was more of a mother to Khalid than Grandma, and she hated it. She hated that she could not totally infiltrate my relationship with Khalid.

"Khalid, take your bath and get ready for bed! Thandie, don't get on the phone at all. You're grounded!"

"For how long?"

"Maybe until the next millennium," she walked out and slammed my bedroom door. I heard the phone ring and ran into the kitchen.

"Thandisha is grounded, and don't call here again!" Andreas and Ayanna were the only people that called me. I knew she was not talking to Ayanna so harshly. She loves Ayanna and thinks she is a good influence. I knew it was Andreas.

"Grandma, why did you do that?"

"Girl, you better get out of my face!" I went back to my room and slammed my door. When Grandma went to sleep, I went to Khalid's room.

"What took you so long Thandie? I'm sleepy."

"Well stay in your own bed."

"No."

"Shut up and come on if you're coming." I then went into the kitchen to get the phone. I connected the phone in my room. Khalid took his usual place at the foot of the bed.

He answered the phone on the first ring.

"Thandisha?"

"Yeah it's me." I had been crying. My nasal passages were clogged.

"Are you okay?"

"Yeah Grandma placed me on restriction. She knows I lied about visiting Ayanna. She knows we were together. I miss you."

"Yeah me too, I guess you can't go tomorrow?"

"I'll meet you at the corner at 9 am."

"I love you."

"I love you too." I hung up the phone and called Ayanna. She answered the phone on the second ring.

"I know this is you Thandisha. Girl, your Grandma came down here mad as hell. Where were you?"

"With Andreas; Guess what? I did it."

"You did what?"

"It."

"No girl. What did it feel like?"

"Ayanna, you never did it before?"

"Hell no." I was surprised. "I flirt with niggahs, but I ain't ready to give up the booty. My daddy would die. What did it feel like?"

"Nothing," I regretted telling her. I thought she had done it before.

"Did it hurt?"

"Hell yea like pure hell, but it was a sweet pain though."

"What you mean sweet?" Ayanna laughed.

"I don't know; it was sweet. Oh yeah guess what? Andreas has an apartment."

"Get out of here."

"Yeah. I'm supposed to go shopping with him tomorrow to buy furniture to decorate it. He said he is going to spend $1000.00 on decorating."

"Where did he get that kind of money?"

"He works."

"Oh yeah; I forgot."

"I have to sneak out of the house. I am already in trouble. I lied to Grandma when I was with Andreas today and told her I was with you."

"Yeah I know; she came over looking for you. I tried to lie for you, but momma was right behind me. They don't let you lie for your friends even though they used to when they were our age."

"I am not going to bible class with them on Sunday. I'll tell her I am sick."

"What are you going to do if she gets back and you're not home?"

"She won't; I'll make sure I get back before she does. She won't get back until 2:30 or 3:00. They always fellowship after bible class anyway." We talked about nothing for an hour before hanging up the phone. I crept back in the kitchen and reconnected the phone.

At 7:00 a.m., as usual, Grandma knocked on the door; and as usual, she scolded Khalid for not sleeping in his room. Even though I hated when she yelled at Khalid, I understand that he is too old to sleep with me. Though he sleeps at the foot of the bed and I sleep at the head, at fourteen, he should be comfortable sleeping alone. Khalid left without saying anything and went to the bathroom to shower. She came back in my room demanding I get ready for bible class. I grabbed the bottom of my stomach, kneeled over, and rolled across the bed.

"Grandma, I'm sick. I don't feel well."

"I don't care if you're sick; get up!"

I sat on the bed. I was slow doing everything. I was determined to make her angry, so she would tell me to leave her alone. Grandma was never late anywhere.

At 7:15, I was making my bed. I was in the shower at 7:25. I knew she would be ready to leave at 7:30. When she came in my room, I was beginning to iron my shirt.

"You ain't ready yet?"

"I'm almost ready."

"Come on Khalid; I am ready to go. Thandisha, you will just have to stay home. I am not going to be late because of your slow ass."

"Grandma, I'm almost ready."

"Well we're not waiting." I put an *I don't believe you're doing this to me* look on my face. She fell for it. She and Khalid left without me.

When they left, I quickly called Andreas to tell him to come to the house instead of meeting me at the corner. I cleaned my room, completed my chores, and got dressed. I put on a pretty beige linen sundress that was loose fitting but still showed what little figure I had. I felt glamorous like a movie star. It was a change; I was coming alive. Actually, I was now feeling instead of simply being. I was now sharing a life with someone, and it felt good. I knew I was being dishonest, but I had to go.

I heard the doorbell. I opened the door and greeted him with a kiss, as he entered the house. He walked in the house, looked around, and focused on the paintings on the wall.

"Did you draw these too?"

"Of course," I smiled; I was always proud of my art. The pictures were beautiful. Some of my pictures were colorful;

others were dark and gloomy. I don't know how I started drawing, but my art was an expression of feelings I couldn't verbalize.

"I have some pictures for your apartment, but they need frames." I grabbed my portfolio, and we left.

"Where are we going?"

"Let's go to the north side. I know I won't get very much, but I don't want a cheap look."

"What kind of look do you want?"

"I don't know just nothing cheap."

"So I guess you want a masculine, macho look?"

"Well I really don't know. I'm sure you will be spending time there too. So what ever you decide." I smiled. I liked that he included me and made me a part of his world.

I went with a neutral tone; we found a beige sofa bed for $500.00 and a matching cream rug. We went to a discount store and purchased blinds and an inexpensive dinette set.

"Wow, you're a good shopper."

"I got it from my momma. My momma was an economical shopper, and she had good taste in furniture." I surprised myself. I never spoke of my mother. She was always on my mind, but I could never verbalize my feelings for her. I put That Day, and everything associated with it, behind me.

"How much do we have left baby?" He had given me the money to pay for the merchandise. I opened my bag. We had been to a few stores, and I lost count of the money.

"We have $236.00 and some change." We drove across town to Coy Country Thrift Store. He didn't want to go, but I loved thrift stores. Upon entering the store, I saw the chair.

"That's it." He looked as if he didn't see it.

"Where?" He looked around the store and still didn't see it.

"Over there," I pointed to the chair and matching ottoman. I walked over to the chair. He reluctantly followed me.

It was mauve with big claw feet. The ottoman was oversized with matching claw feet.

"Look it's only sixty dollars." It was obvious; he wasn't impressed. I remember momma used to say that every room should have an antique.

"Trust me; you're going to love this." We paid for the chair and placed it in the trunk of the car. We had to tie the trunk down, as the chair was too big.

"What about dinnerware and linens?"

"I have dinnerware and linen. I have been planning to move for quite some time, so I have been buying stuff here and there. I plan early baby." He placed a gentle, moist kiss on my forehead.

We walked next door to a fast food restaurant for lunch. I was midway into eating my burger when I noticed that it was 1:00. I was already in trouble. I didn't want to make it worse.

"Andreas, look at the time." He looked at his watch.

"Damn baby, I have to get you home." He flagged down the waitress and paid our bill. He drove so fast that I was sure he would get a ticket. Surprisingly, however, we made it back to Grandma's house without being pulled over by flashing, blue lights.

"Babe, I am going to go home and put up the blinds. I guess I'll clean up and put that ugly chair in the apartment." I gave him a long, passionate kiss. I was always sad when he left me. I went into the house, put on my baggy jeans and T-shirt, and went back to sleep.

I heard the door open; it was Grandma, Khalid, and Aunt Mary. Khalid came to my room as usual. He opened the door without knocking.

"Thandie."

"Yeah!" I snapped at him.

"Nothing," he closed the door. I immediately felt guilty. I knew Khalid was dependent on me; sometimes I liked his dependency; at other times, I hated it. Sometimes it was more than I could handle. I got up and went in Khalid's room. I rarely went in his room because he was always in mine.

"Khalid!" He didn't say anything. I went over to his bed and pushed his shoulder.

"You want me to make you some French toast?"

"You gonna put some cream cheese filling in it?" He continued to face the wall.

"Yeah," he turned over, sat up and gave me a big hug.

"I'm sorry Khalid."

We went in the kitchen. Khalid immediately grabbed the French Bread from the cupboard. I cut the bread into four, thick slices. Khalid was excited. It takes very little to make him happy, but sometimes, I don't even have a little to give. He cracked the eggs while I mixed the vanilla flavor and cinnamon into the cream cheese and sugar.

"Thandie, can you make banana syrup?"

"Look and see if we have bananas." I hoped that we didn't, but of course, Khalid found some. I melted the brown sugar and butter then sliced the bananas and added them to the mixture.

"What are you guys making?" I should have known Aunt Mary would come into the kitchen. She always came in the kitchen when she smelled my cooking.

"French toast with banana syrup. Would you like some Aunt Mary?"

"Yeah that sounds good."

"It sure smells good in here." Grandma came into the kitchen. She must have been lying down because one side of her afro was flat, and her face had the imprint of her bedspread.

"What is that white topping you are spreading on the bread Thandie?"

"It is a mixture of cream cheese, vanilla, and frozen cool whip." I finished making the French toast in the midst of

51

Grandma, Khalid, and Aunt Mary and topped it with the banana syrup.

"Thandie, this is delicious."

"Thanks Grandma."

"Baby, do you mind making these for the bible class brunch next Saturday?"

"Sure Aunt Mary," I loved when Aunt Mary ate my cooking; she made me feel special. Khalid wasn't saying anything. He was busy filling his mouth. I loved cooking desserts, pastries, and cheesecakes because I enjoyed the compliments that I always received when they are eaten.

After we finished our French toast, I washed dishes and cleaned the kitchen. I read the newspaper in the den while Aunt Mary, Khalid, and Grandma watched television. This was a nice rarity, as I was always in my room when Grandma was in the den because she was usually getting on me about something; sometimes so harshly that Aunt Mary would have to intervene.

"Grandma, can you drop me off at the mall tomorrow morning? I want to get a job."

"Thandie, you really don't need a job."

"Yes I do Grandma. I want to make my own money."

"I really think it's good that she wants to work; some of these kids today don't want to do anything but drink and use drugs." Aunt Mary agreed with me. Grandma still didn't say anything.

"Well Thelma, baby, I can drop her off."

"I can ride the bus back Grandma." She really didn't have a leg to stand on because she did not have to do anything to help me get this job I would fictitiously look for.

"You better not be up to anything."

"I'm not Grandma. I need a job."

"No Thandie, you want a job."

"I'm 17 years old Grandma, and I need to save my own money. I won't do anything that I am not supposed to do."

Aunt Mary came to pick me up at 10:00. Andreas and I made plans to meet at the Taco Stand at 10:30. The ride with Aunt Mary was peaceful. I enjoyed spending time with her alone. She was very easy going. She didn't mind when I changed her radio station from the oldies to my favorite hiphop station. Though she was older than Grandma, she was more modern thinking. She had a much more realistic view of my teenage life. She didn't place unrealistic expectations on me.

"I hear you have a boyfriend."

"Yeah I do. His name is Andreas. He graduated this year."

"Really that's good so many of our young, black men don't even make it out of high school." I truly get tired of the negative comments people make about black youth. I don't know "the young black men" Aunt Mary spoke of. Everyone I know graduated from high school. "Is he nice?"

"Oh Aunt Mary he is so sweet. He talks to me about everything, his dreams, goals and his family."

"You think you love him don't you?" I didn't want to tell her too much. I knew that she would tell Grandma any and every thing.

"Well I don't know if I love him." I lied. "But he is very nice. Grandma won't even talk to him."

"She'll come around." When we arrived at the mall, I tried to be inconspicuous in my search for Andreas' car.

"Aunt Mary, let me out at the front entrance to the mall." She reached in her hip pocket, pulled out her wallet, and gave me $20.00. I grabbed my backpack that contained my jeans and T-shirt and thanked Aunt Mary for the money.

I walked to the Taco Stand; Andreas was sitting at a table sipping on a soft drink. He stood up and greeted me with a kiss. He took my book bag, and we walked to his car. As always, he opened the door and secured me in the seat belt.

"Guess what? The furniture is already in the apartment. We need to arrange everything. I found one of those tall floor lamps." He sounded excited.

"Oh you did? So you went shopping without me huh?" He didn't say anything; he simply looked at me and smiled.

The apartment was cool from the window unit. I could tell he attempted to arrange the furniture. Everything was totally out of balance. He placed all of the furniture on one side of the wall.

"What do you think?"

"I can tell you tried." He laughed.

"Go to the frame store, get the pictures framed, and I'll have a surprise when you get back."

I moved the sofa, so it separated the breakfast nook from the living area. I placed the lamp on the back of the couch to provide light for the dining area as well as the sitting area. I placed the antique chair cater-cornered on the wall and positioned it for easy viewing of the television and placed the throw rug in front of the sofa. It was beautiful. He came back with the framed prints and Chinese food.

"Wow, this is great; thank you baby." We ate the food and watched television. I sat close to him. I could feel a hard bulge in his pants. We both ignored it. We lay down and took a brief nap. At 2:00, he awakened and dressed for work. I changed back into my skirt.

We drove to my house in silence. Initially, we passed the house to ensure we didn't see Grandma.

"I get off work at 11:00 call me at 11:30." I kissed him, went in the house, and called Ayanna.

"Girl, where have you been? I have been calling you all morning."

"I went to decorate Andreas' apartment; he had some of my drawings professionally framed for his apartment."

"Girl, I bet it's nice."

"It's real nice. You want to see it?"

"I would love to see it."

"Ask your mother if you can use the car."

"Where is the apartment?"

"It's in the West End."

"I am not allowed to drive on the freeway. My dad says that I need more experience." Ayanna was obedient and honest. Unlike me, she was grounded. I looked for things and people outside of me to make me whole. She was solid on the inside and very secure with herself. Ayanna was not influenced by peer pressure. In fact, she was always the trendsetter.

"I'll ask Dee to take us."

"Won't she tell your momma? I don't want Grandma to know. If she knew Andreas had an apartment, she would really be on my case."

"Girl, please, as much dirt as I have on Dee. I think not." Dee and Ayanna picked me up, and we rode to the West End. We could tell Dee was mad, but we didn't care. Ayanna and I sat in the back seat with Dee's two kids in the middle. We talked about Andreas and Devontae, her new love. We gossiped about who was pregnant and who was cheating on whom; we were totally oblivious to Dee and her attitude. We were engulfed in our own world.

It was a twenty-minute drive from Grandma's house to Andreas' apartment. I was excited and proud showing it off.

"This is it?" Ayanna was totally unimpressed.

"Girl, wait until you see the inside." The apartment was still cool although it was ninety degrees outside. Andreas was neat and clean. Everything was orderly, and in its place.

"This is nice. Are those your drawings?" I knew Ayanna would see the beauty once we were inside.

"Yeah and you know it." The paintings were beautiful. Framing them was a good idea.

"Thandisha you have real talent."

55

"What can I say?" I was flattered by the compliment. Ayanna has always known that I am an artist, but we spend most of the time talking about her and what boyfriend she liked the most, or what she was going to wear to this party or that party. I have shown her my work many times; I guess the fact that I was a great artist never sunk in.

We were startled when Dee came inside with the kids.

"This is nice."

"Thanks Dee."

"This is your boyfriend's apartment?"

"Yes, this is it."

"Wow, he has nice art. I bet he paid a fortune for it."

"Thandisha painted all of them."

"Thandisha, this is good."

"So what does he do?"

"Who?"

"Your boyfriend, what kind of work does he do?"

"He works at Tyler manufacturing, and he has his own lawn maintenance business." Dee appeared impressed.

"I hear they make big bucks at Tyler's."

"And he has a girlfriend named Thandisha. You know the girl standing next to me with the key." Ayanna pointed at me while rolling her eyes at Dee. I didn't know how to take Dee's comment, but Ayanna obviously did.

Dee dropped both of us off at my house. Grandma's car was gone. I looked forward to enjoying a peaceful house. As I entered the house, I heard the television in the den. Khalid was stretched out in the middle of the floor watching television. I hated when Grandma left him alone. I know that he is old enough to stay home alone. But sometimes he is still afraid to be in the house alone.

Grandma came in the house smiling. She was always happy when Ayanna visited. It was a rare event because I was usually at her house. I took advantage of her happy demeanor and asked permission to spend the night with Ayanna. I couldn't believe it; she allowed me to spend the night. This was quite unusual. Although she was okay with me visiting Ayanna, she never liked for me to spend the night. I told her we were going skating.

"Just come home before 11:00. I have an appointment at 12:30 tomorrow."

"Okay Grandma." I knew that I wasn't going to be spending the night with Ayanna. When we got to her house, I asked her if Dee would take me to Andreas' house if I gave her money for gas.

"Girl, are you crazy? You're going too far Thandisha."

"Ayanna, I love Andreas. He loves me. What's wrong with that?"

"Thandisha, don't you think you're going too fast? What about college? You know we are supposed to be roommates and pledge a sorority together."

"I don't want to go to college. Ayanna, I want to become a world-renowned artist. I'm very talented. Andreas said that we're going to sell some of my paintings on consignment."

"Why is everything Andreas this and Andreas that? Whatever happened to having fun, enjoying life, liking boys and going to backyard BBQ's?"

"Nothing aren't we going skating? I still like having fun and hanging out with you."

"Oh, we're really going skating?"

"Yeah," Ayanna eyes lit up like a child's on Christmas day. She smiled and hugged me.

"Oh my God I don't have anything to wear. You should have said something earlier; we could have gone to the mall. Come on girl let's go on over to my house. I need to wash my hair and find something to wear." Ayanna paused and stared at my hair.

"Why don't you ever wear your hair loose? I tell you what I'll wash your hair and wrap it. Girl we're gonna be so fine tonight."

We opened the door and found Dee in the den talking on the phone and smoking cigarettes.

"Dee, you know that you're not supposed to smoke in here." Dee waved her hand brushing Ayanna off and continued her conversation with the cigarette in her hand blowing the smoke directly towards Ayanna.

"Ain't no use some folks just won't do right." We went into the kitchen where Ayanna began the tedious task of taking my hair down.

"Thandisha, you have a lot of hair.......Hey Dee." She screamed Dee's name so loud I had to cover my ears. I hated the way Ayanna talked to Dee. It was very obvious that Ayanna did not have the respect for Dee that is given to an older sibling. You could tell by the tone Ayanna used when she spoke to Dee, and she never had anything nice to say to or about Dee.

"What?" I could tell by the way Dee responded to Ayanna that she knew that she was not respected.

"Where's your gel?" Ayanna stood still waiting for Dee to respond. "I know that heifer heard me." I am sure she heard Ayanna too. I wanted to tell Ayanna that maybe if she spoke to her with a little more respect, she may respond. Dee didn't respond; she totally ignored Ayanna.

"Sit here for a second Thandisha." She dashed out in a huff with major attitude as if she were on route to a street fight. She came back into the kitchen with a large jar of hair gel. I hoped that she had not planned on using it on my hair. I hated putting gel in my hair. I honestly didn't see the point. It cakes up and leaves dingy, dark flakes.

"Thandisha, you need to cut some of this stuff." She washed my hair and totally ignored my protest against applying the gel to my hair. She wrapped my hair around my head; it took

58

forever. I sat under the dryer for over two hours before my hair was dry. Ayanna combed it down and used a flat iron to straighten it. I looked in the mirror. I hated my hair down because I looked too much like momma.

"Ayanna, I really don't like wearing my hair loose."

"Girl please, it looks nice." She made a small part on the side allowing hair to fall on both of my shoulders.

"Thandisha, you should wear your hair like this more often. You're very pretty." We went into the den. Dee looked at me with evil eyes and gave me an unwarranted eye roll. Ayanna obviously saw it. "Don't pay her any attention. That child has some serious issues."

I put on my tight, hip hugger jeans and a cute snug fitting crop shirt. If I may say so myself, I looked good. Although I am still slim, my hips are rounding and my behind is beginning to stick out more. The jeans truly accented my figure. Dee dropped us off at the skate center. She didn't say a word to us during the entire trip.

"Dee, I will be ready at 11:30."

"Yeah whatever."

"Don't be late either Dee." Ayanna slammed the car door; I was surprised the window did not shatter.

"I hate that bitch. Damn, if she wasn't my sister, I would not even talk to her stupid ass."

"You really don't hate her Ayanna. I think they call it sibling rivalry."

"I guess I really don't hate her dumb ass, but she gets on my damn nerves."

We walked in the skate center. The music was full of bass and loud enough that you could feel the vibrations in your chest. Everyone from school was there. We skated to the latest rap songs and old R&B. I could not keep up with Ayanna. She was very popular with the boys, and she liked the fact a lot of boys liked her. I could care less about being popular or hanging with the in-crowd. Andreas was the only guy that interested me. I only wanted to hang out with him. In fact, I had become bored looking at Ayanna and her entourage. I paged him, and waited by the pay phone for him to call me back.

He called back at 11:10; I told him that I was at the skate center and Grandma thinks that I am spending the night with Ayanna. I didn't have to say anything else.

"I'll be right there."

Andreas and Dee both arrived at 11:30. Dee got out of the car with hoochie shorts and a two-size, too small, tight tank top and walked over to Andreas' side of the car. I didn't like the way she looked at him while blowing the smoke from her cigarette in his face.

"Hi I'm Dee, Ayanna's older sister." Of course, she emphazied "older." "I saw your apartment, and it really looks nice. Do you mind if I ask you something?" She paused, batting her fake eyelashes while blowing smoke in Andreas' face. "How much is the rent?" He looked kind of surprised.

"$550.00, but that includes utilities."

"Are there any vacancies?"

"Yeah I think so. I'll give Thandisha the number to the owners, and she'll give it to you."

"I'd really appreciate that; I would appreciate that a lot." She gave him a seductive smile before she slowly turned around and walked to her car. Andreas didn't appear to notice her darkened cheeks that subtly hung from her tight shorts. The car was abnormally silent.

"What was that all about?"

"I wanted Ayanna to see the apartment. She's not allowed to drive on the freeway, so Dee gave us a ride." He didn't say anything.

"Are you mad? I mean did I do something wrong?"

"I could never be mad at you." He took my hand and placed it against his cheek reassuring me with a soft kiss. I removed my seat belt and sat in the middle of the car with my head on his shoulder.

The apartment, as usual, was clean and orderly. We walked in, and he immediately turned on the air conditioner. We ate cereal, chips, and drank soda while watching television.

"The only thing that's missing is groceries. You need some food in here."

"Why? I can't cook."

"I can. I can cook for you." I snuggled up next to him.

"How about we get up in the morning and go to the store."

"Okay but I have to be home at 11:00."

"Well we'll get up extra early."

He put on a jazz CD and pulled out the sofa bed. Soft music was exactly what I needed. I loved Andreas so much. I finally felt loved again, and it felt so good. We were kissing passionately; he turned on the light and reached for his wallet.

"Damn!"

"What?"

"I don't have any more jimmies." I pulled him back on top of me grinding against his manhood kissing him with a passion that I didn't know I had. I was scared, but I wanted him to touch me so badly. I felt so alive when he touched me. He kissed my breast and massaged the mound between my thighs. He entered me, and this time it didn't hurt.

"Baby, you feel so good." He kissed me everywhere. He pulled out of me and then gave me pleasure with his mouth. When he entered me again, I was on fire. Then something happened; I actually had an orgasm. The sensation between my legs was so powerful that I moaned, squealed and called his name pulling him closer without being totally cognizant of my actions; then he moaned and shivered with perspiration pouring out of him, dripping onto my face and rolling down onto the pillow. "I love you baby; damn I love you." He pulled out of me and climaxed rubbing his manhood against my stomach. We lay silently in each other's arms several minutes before we spoke again.

"Your hair is pretty loose; well it was pretty." He laughed. It was soaked with his perspiration. The ends were beginning to curl totally destroying the new look Ayanna had given me.

"I'm sorry about today. I could tell you were mad that I brought Ayanna and Dee here."

"I wasn't mad."

"Yes you were."

"Well I was uncomfortable but not mad. I have lived in the projects all my life, with nothing but people around. I like my space away from people that's what that was about. I wasn't exactly mad."

"It won't happen again." We kissed, talked, made love and talked some more.

"Did I tell you I got a small business license yesterday?"

"No you didn't tell me."

"Well I did. Now I can bid on city contracts. They have a bid list at city hall for different government contracts. If I can get two bids next year, then I'm in there. I'll buy more equipment. These are year round contracts too. I'll save the checks from my business and live off my paycheck. I know your grandmother still probably won't like me, but she'll see I am a hard working man. She will see that I will treat you right, and I can take care of you as good as any man." I really didn't know what all of that meant, but it sounded good to me.

"Did you get any more of your paintings ready?"

"Yeah I did."

"I'll take them to be framed, and we'll try and sell them on consignment." I loved Andreas because he made my life a priority also. He made the things that were important to me important to him. We talked until we fell asleep.

I awakened with him shaking me. "Thandisha wake up; baby wake up."

"Hey when are you going to trust me enough to tell me about it?"

"About what?"

"About you." I sat up in the bed still crying. I didn't know how to say it. I didn't have the words anymore. I don't even know if I could remember it all. It seemed as if That Day happened a lifetime ago. I did everything in my power to put That Day out of my mind, and now he wants me to tell him about it.

"Say it anyway you want to say it."

"Something very bad happened when I was a little girl." He looked at me waiting for more

"When Khalid and I were younger, somebody killed our mother. I was there. I saw her. I saw the blood. The blood was on me. I saw him." I couldn't talk anymore; the words wouldn't come. I looked at him hoping that I had given him enough information.

"That must have been hard. Did they catch the guy who did it?"

"Yeah he is in prison. I don't know which one, but he is in prison."

"Well you don't need to know where he is. At least you know that he can't hurt you anymore." He lay on his back, pulled me close, and softly rubbed my hair. I laid my head in his chest. The rhythmic sound of his heartbeat was hypnotic, inducing a sound sleep.

I awakened at sunrise, but I was so relaxed that I went back to sleep. When I awakened again, it was 10:00. I pushed Andreas' shoulder back and forth about five times before he woke up. I quickly put my clothes on, pulled a rubber band from my purse, and pulled my hair back. He made the bed and sat on the sofa watching me.

"You're pretty Thandisha. I wish you didn't have to leave." I walked to the sofa and gave him a long, passionate kiss.

"Me either."

"You said your grandmother has an appointment."

"Yeah I have to hang out with my brother."

"Why don't I pick you and your brother up after she leaves? We can go grocery shopping and have lunch before I go to work."

"Yeah that will work, but I have to go now."

He let me out of the car at Ayanna's house. I checked to make sure Grandma had not called then I quickly walked home.

As usual, Khalid was waiting in the den for me. He opened the door before I could ring the doorbell.

"Did you have a nice time Thandie?"

"Yeah it was real nice." I went into my room, watched television and waited for Grandma to leave.

"Khalid! Get dressed!"

"Why?"

"Because I said so." He went into his room and changed into a pair of baggy shorts and matching over-sized shirt. I called Andreas to come and pick us up. Khalid was more responsive to Andreas than before. They talked about the Bulls, the Pacers, and the Lakers, Khalid's favorite basketball team. I didn't know Khalid knew so much about basketball. I was impressed.

We went to the grocery store and then to the apartment to put the food away. We drove downtown and ate lunch. I ordered a grilled chicken salad. Andreas ordered steak and baked potato, and Khalid had the usual, cheeseburger and fries. By the time we finished our meals, it was time for him to take us home and go to work. I always hated when he had to take me home. Andreas and I sat in the car. Khalid went into the house while I kissed Andreas good-bye.

"I hate leaving you Thandisha."

"Me too. Pick me up tonight at 12:00."

"What?" He looked surprised.

"You heard me. I'll sneak out of the window."

"You sure?" I took his hand and placed it inside of my panties. "Um huh." We both laughed.

Later in the evening, Ayanna came over, and we watched television and engaged in our usual teenage gossip. Actually she did all of the talking. I was listening but not really paying attention, but since she talked so much, she didn't even notice.

"You talk to that boy today?" I didn't like the way she said "that boy."

"Yeah of course."

"Why did I bother to ask?"

"Thandisha, you're changing." What she really meant was that she was concerned because she was no longer the center of my attention.

"Ayanna, I'm in love. I want to be with him every moment all of the time. I miss him right now even. I love the way he smells even when he's just coming from work."

"Thandisha, you're way too young for all that. When we go to college, you'll meet so many people that Andreas won't even matter." I was tired of her telling me that I was going to college. I have told her a hundred times that I have no intention of going to college. I'm going to be an excellent cook and a great artist. Art is natural for me. I don't have to go to college to be an artist.

"I don't think so; I need him."

"Whatever, look at Dee, she was the same way stuck on some boy. She got married then had those damn brats. Now look at her." I was waiting to hear more. I wanted to tell her that the only thing wrong with Dee is that she has a very judgmental sister and a harsh daddy that wants to make her feel bad for the rest of her life because she got married without his approval.

"And?"

"And? Hell, she's living back at home. Momma and daddy begged her to go to school. Oh, but not her grown ass! She had to marry Eddie, but she got hers. When he beat her the last time, she almost died. Look at her; she's lost. She has been to cosmetology school, secretary school, and bookkeeping school. She is so damn confused; she's just a damn embarrassment."

"That's mean Ayanna. Sometimes you can make all of the right decisions and everything can still go wrong. I learned a long time ago that we really are not in control. We just think that we are. We are totally powerless; believe me I know." I saw tears forming in her eyes. I have known Ayanna for over five years, and I have never seen her cry.

"Dee has always taken all of the attention. She always has some damn crazy drama in her life. Always some outlandish shit too that requires both momma and daddy's attention. I'm sick of her. When she moved back home, momma assumed April was going to share my room. But daddy put his foot down and said that April had to share a room with her mother." Ayanna and I rarely talked about ourselves. We always talked about other people. I didn't know how much she resented Dee, but it seemed to me that Dee should have been resenting Ayanna. Ayanna was obviously her dad's favorite. She had his undivided attention.

"Besides, Thandisha, what kind of future does Andreas have? What kind of life can he offer you? Hell, he cuts grass for a living. What kind of life is that?" She was beginning to piss me off.

"So what Ayanna, he makes an honest living. A college degree doesn't mean everything. There are plenty of people who never go to college and manage to earn a good living."

"Yeah but how many people do you know who have good jobs without a degree?" I couldn't answer her. I wanted to remind her that her father has a MBA, but hasn't been able to find a job in his field for years. Yes he still works in an office, but he did not need a MBA to be an insurance adjuster.

I was grateful Ayanna changed the subject and refocused on herself. To be honest, I was mad as hell at her for blatantly insulting Andreas. I listened to Ayanna talk about some new guy named Keith for the next two hours. It was getting late, and I wanted to get ready to go over to Andreas' house. I kept yawning hoping that she would get the hint, but she didn't. We talked, rather she talked, an hour longer until her pager went off. She quickly grabbed the pager from her back pocket.

"Oooh girl I have to go home. This is Darryl. Maybe he will take me out tonight." I wanted to inquire about Devontae and Keith, but didn't want to delay her departure. I walked her to the door, and we said our goodbyes.

I didn't want to shower; I wanted to wait until I got to Andreas' because it made me feel as if it was my place too. It felt like we were a couple living together. I went and got Khalid at 9:00, so he could sleep in my bed. I sat and watched him sleep for a while. He was growing up, and he was so handsome. Khalid was such a good brother. I was surprised at how he adjusted to living without momma. It was easier, for some reason, for Grandma to love him than it was for her to love me.

Before I left out of the window, I placed two pillows next to him. I walked down the street toward Ayanna's house until I saw the blinking lights. I jogged towards the car, but I really wanted to run. I was always excited when I saw him. I gave him my usual kiss and slid in the middle of the seat close to him.

We were quiet the entire drive to his place. We were both tired. I wanted to climb on his back and be carried inside of the apartment. He was so tired that we both probably would have ended up on the ground. When we got inside, we quickly made the bed, undressed and went to sleep.

We were awakened by a loud, hard knock at the door; I glanced at the clock. It was 4:00 am. It was Jazmyne, Andreas' younger sister. One of her eyes was swollen shut and her lip was busted and coated with dried blood.

"Damn girl, what happened to you?" Andreas tightly wrapped his arms around Jazymyne and escorted her to the chair. I only had on one of Andreas' t-shirts, so I kept the covers pulled close.

"I'm tired of that niggah." Jazmyne was not very attractive, and she looked worse crying.

"Sit down girl. Tell me what happened." He went in the kitchen and got an ice pack for her face.

"It went like dis." I hated the way Jazmyne talked. Her sentences were always filled with dis niggah dat niggah and the way she sucked her teeth when she talked drove me crazy.

"You know Keekee started slangin." He shook his head in disgust. I didn't know what slangin was. Jazmyne spoke an entirely different language. "Well he just doing it so we can get our own spot. Anyway he was trying to sell a slab. When he looked at his stash, he said some was missing. Since I was the only one in the car, he accused me." He stood, grabbed Jazmyne, and pulled her to her feet.

"Girl, I know you ain't smoking that shit." I had no idea what "that shit" was. She didn't answer; she continued to talk.

"He made me take off all of my clothes in front of Jerry, Tae, and DeeDee dem and searched me and shit; and when he didn't find it, he jumped on me." She started crying again.

"Keekee should be tired of me kicking his ass." Andreas slid into his jeans and grabbed a shirt.

"Bro wait; don't go. He packing and shit."
Andreas pushed her out of the way and slammed the door.

Jazmyne and I had nothing in common to talk about; we occasionally looked at one another and smiled. After sitting in the chair for a few minutes, Jazmyne reached in her hair and pulled out a white pebble.

"Look don't tell my brother; it would kill him."

She smoked a cigarette placing the ashes on a pipe. She broke off a piece of the pebble and lit it with a lighter and inhaled the smoke from the pipe. She immediately stopped crying and started talking as if nothing happened.

"I hope my brother don't find Keekee. He done beat Keekee so many times; it's a shame. Eventually, somebody is going to get hurt."

"Why does he hit you?"

"He is so crazy. He loves me too much. Don't want me out of his sight." She looked around at the place nodding her head up and down with approval.

"Dis real nice. Dem some real pretty pictures."

"Thank you."

"Thank you? Oh you must live here or something?"

"No, I painted the pictures."

"Oh girl these are real nice. Um huh." I hated the way this girl talked. I couldn't wait until Andreas got back so that he could take me home and get me away from her.

"So you the reason my brother doesn't come home no more. You putting that thang on him right huh gull." She started to gyrate her hips. I was speechless. I simply looked at her.

"Me and Keekee trying to get our own place. Hell I'm tired of getting fucked in the car and on the side of buildings and shit." I sat still and continued to stare at her. I've never had a conversation with anyone like this before.

"This is real nice. Gull don't hurt my brother. He a real good dude. He really is um huh. You're only his second girlfriend. Don't you know Katanya Thomas? You know that girl who had the baby last year." I didn't know her, but I knew this would not stop her from telling me whatever it was she was going to tell me. "Well anyway they went together for along time. You know like since jr. high and shit. She got pregnant. My brother thought it was his cause you know he thought she was down with him and shit. Well you know Andreas black as

midnight. Her ass is just as black as his. The baby came out
light skinned with hazel eyes and shit. He still didn't want to
believe it. He was saying something about maybe the genes went
way back. The fool didn't believe it until the blood test came
back. He was so hurt gull. You know he didn't beat that bitch
ass. Shit, but I did. Don't nobody fuck with my brother. Hell."
I felt relieved when I heard him place his key in the door.
He looked tired.
"You might as well take me home. It's 5:30."
"Oh baby why?"
"I need to get home before Grandma awakens; plus your
sister needs to get some rest."
"I sho' do gull. I'm tired of getting my ass beat, thrown
out of moving cars and stripped searched and shit. Damn that
fool is crazy." Jazmyne was laughing. I didn't see the humor.
Andreas looked at her shaking his head in disgust. He looked
sad.
I changed into my clothes. He drove almost in complete
silence.
"What's wrong Andreas?" He looked at me and smiled.
"Nothing baby everything is alright as long as I have
you." He turned the lights off before reaching the house. I
kissed him good-bye. I was tired and sleepy. I crawled back
through the window; Khalid was in the same position. I put on
my pajamas and went to sleep.
When I awakened, it was 11:30 am. I couldn't believe
Grandma allowed me sleep this late. I awakened and called
Andreas.
"Hello." He always sounded so sexy in the morning.
"Hey."
"What's up baby?" I loved the way he said baby.
"You."
"I'm sorry about the thing with my sister this morning.
She has somewhat of a dramatic life."

"It's okay."

"No it's not. That's one of the reasons I moved. I wanted to get away from my family and their crazy drama and make a world of my own. I can't seem to escape." He paused. "Fuck it. I'm going to make it anyway. Hell I got to make it." Although I didn't totally understand exactly what he was talking about, I knew it was about pain. I had a lot of my own; it maintained its place behind every happy, blessed event in my life. Like a dark shadow it was determined to stay affixed to my life. I didn't really know how to help him. I couldn't verbalize my own pain, but it was there deep inside of me. I couldn't touch it, but I knew it was there.

School starts next week, and I dreaded it. How would I see Andreas? When would we have the time? With him doing his lawn business during the day and working in the afternoon, it really didn't leave very much time for me. I didn't know how, but the time would be made. It was essential. I needed him like I needed lungs to breathe.

Ayanna was excited, as usual, about school. I walked to her house like I do every year, and she shows me the new clothes she bought for school. She meticulously takes each piece out of the bag as if it were a precious jewel and then cautiously returns it after she admires each piece with me. Of course, she has never asked me about my clothes, which was okay. I was never really into the school-shopping thing. I shopped all of the time. Whenever I wanted to buy clothes, I would simply buy them.

I didn't see Andreas for the first three days of school then Wednesday night I couldn't take it. I paged him at work.

"Hello," it didn't take him long to return my call.

"May I speak to Thandisha?"

"Hey it's me."

"Hey baby I miss you."

"Me too, Pick me up tonight."

"Are you sure? What about school? Won't you be tired in the morning?"

"Yeah. I sure hope so." We both laughed. "I'll call you when I know Grandma is asleep." I didn't get Khalid. I was trying to teach him to sleep comfortable in his bed.

I pushed up the window, crawled out of it and quietly closed it. I walked down the street until I saw the lights blink on and off. I got in the car; we sat still for a minute hugging and kissing. I didn't know how much I missed him until I saw him.

"I have a present for you."

"Really? I was expecting a present but next week for my birthday." We drove holding and kissing at every red light and every stop sign. When we got to his apartment, I pulled out the sofa bed before I showered. I always finish before he does. He has to wash everything three or four times. I lather myself very good one time, and I am done.

He came to the side of the bed and dropped the towel before climbing into bed. He reached over to the lamp table and pulled out a small, velvet box.

"I wanted to wait and give this to you for your birthday, but I was too excited." Inside of the box was a marquis shaped, diamond ring.

"It's only a fourth of a carat, but it's a quality one."
I cried. No one had ever given me anything so special. He took it out of the box and placed it on my finger.

We didn't even look for a condom. I didn't care; neither did he. There was so much to loose and so much to gain. I knew Andreas loved me. I knew I loved him. We were so caught up in the moment that we didn't care about the consequences.

135°
One Hundred and Thirty-five Degrees

By October, my period still had not come. Last month, I threw away sanitary napkins splattered with ketchup to conceal my lack of a monthly flow. Initially, I didn't tell Andreas. I was so sick in the mornings that I would get up early before anyone was awake, go into the bathroom and regurgitate. I was tired all of the time. Most days after school, I went straight to bed and sometimes slept until the next morning.

Finally, I was so sick that instead of going to school, I called Andreas and confessed that I had not had a period in a couple of months.

"What? Are you pregnant?"

"I don't know."

"What do you mean you don't know?"

"I don't fucking know!" I was frustrated, so I hung up the phone. He immediately called back."

"Yeah!"

"Thandisha, don't hang up the damn phone again!" There was a long silence. I was too confused to speak. I guess he was too.

"Look, whatever happens we will handle it. I can't believe that you didn't tell me. What were you thinking?"

"I wasn't thinking."

The next morning, he picked me up at the bus stop, and we went to the health clinic. The results were positive. The nurse gave us pamphlets and information, so we could make an informed decision. We were silent and didn't talk until we were in the car.

"Are you hungry?" The thought of food made me nauseous. I didn't want anything to eat. Andreas stopped at a burger stand. Immediately, the smell of the food turned my stomach. I regurgitated what seemed like everything I had eaten in the last year. He had to eat his burger and onion rings outside of the car. When he finished eating, he quietly got in the car, and we drove to his apartment.

The apartment was nice and cool. He pulled out the sofa bed and covered the mattress with a sheet.

"Baby, lie down." I removed my shoes. He sat next to me and massaged my feet.

"I don't want to have a baby. I don't even know how to take care of myself."

"I know; but it's a little too late. Don't you think? Remember I have eight nieces and three nephews. I've changed diapers. I've done it all. All I am asking is that you have the baby. You can still go to school."

School, I hadn't even thought about school. What would Ayanna say? What would she think? Grandma, Aunt Mary, Khalid what would they think of me?

"I can't go to school like this!"

"Yes hell you can!" He stood up and quickly sat down again. "I make good money. I have a side business that is growing; by next summer, it should be booming. You graduate in seven months. By then, the baby will be here. We can get married. I know this place is small, but we can stay here until the baby comes."

Marriage! Was he crazy? I wasn't ready for marriage. I didn't want to be like my momma.

"Andreas, I'm not ready for marriage; my mother was married very young."

"We're having a baby. We need to get married. Okay I'll tell you what, we can live here together until you're ready." I was tired and totally stressed out. Talking to him didn't help, so I stretched out and fell asleep. When I awakened, he had prepared chicken soup and crackers.

"We're going to have to tell your grandmother." I choked on the soup spraying it in his face.

"Are you crazy?"

"No I'm not crazy. I'm a man, and I'm not hiding behind anything that I have done. I love you, and I am willing to take responsibility for you and my baby."

"I'm not telling Grandma anything." I looked at him like he was absolutely out of his mind. I couldn't believe he was serious about having this baby.

"Now wait a minute Thandisha. Now hold it. No you're right. I'll tell her."

"What?"

"Baby, I have struggled since I was thirteen trying very hard not to be like my father. I'm a man. You're having my baby. I will be responsible for my baby. I will take responsibility for you. I'm not a coward. I'm going to tell your grandmother with or without you." I fell back on the sofa, stretched my body, rolled over, and cried into the pillow. I was afraid. What would Grandma do? What would she say? It was 3:00 and time for me to be getting out of school.

"Why haven't you left for work?"

"I called in sick today." Since I have known Andreas, he has never taken a day off work. I couldn't believe that he was serious about telling Grandma.

"I told you that I was going to talk to your grandmother." I quickly stood up.

75

"No not now. I haven't decided what I am going to do yet." I paced back and forth across the living room.

"Thandisha, you're not killing my baby. If you don't want anything to do with it, I'll have to accept that. But it is my baby too. I'm a man, and I will take full responsibility." I sat down on the sofa.

"Are you coming?"

"No," I could never tell Grandma something like this. He left shaking his head in disgust. He was gone for over two hours. I couldn't sleep. What was Grandma going to say? I anxiously waited for him to return.

He opened the door, and he came inside with three suitcases.

"What's that?"

"Your clothes."

"She put me out?"

"Yes and no."

"She said that she respected me for coming to her like a man. We talked about an hour. She said that she loved you, but she couldn't deal with your being pregnant. I gave her the address and phone number, and she said that she and Khalid would visit this weekend."

"That's all she said?"

"No, she cursed me, talked about my mother and father, and damned me to hell."

"That's it?"

"No she said for you to stay in school, or she would never speak to you again. And she said that you could come and get the rest of your things. She also said that I could come and get some things that belonged to your mother tonight because she said that you are very attached to some of your mother's things."

Andreas unpacked and folded my clothes while I slept. When I awakened, he was watching the evening news.

"Are you hungry?"

"No, I am still a little sick."

"Baby, you need to eat." I didn't feel like eating. I didn't feel like doing much of anything. Andreas borrowed his mentor's truck and went to Grandma's house to get the rest of my things. My favorite piece of furniture was an antique cedar wood armoire that belonged to my mother. It took up a lot of space. The apartment was so small, but I had to have it near me. I placed it on the side of the small foyer that led to the bathroom and used it to hang my clothes.

I was scared; reality was sinking in. I was 18 years old, pregnant, and my most prized possessions were in my boyfriend's apartment. I enjoyed sneaking over here to be with him but actually living with him was scary. Could Grandma really put me out? Wasn't it me and Khalid's house too? I wanted to call Grandma and tell her that I was sorry. I wanted to go home. I was crying uncontrollably by the time Andreas came back in the room. He was with me, but I felt alone.

I looked forward to the weekend. I wanted to see Grandma, Khalid and Aunt Mary. I missed Grandma's house. I missed my little brother, who really wasn't little anymore, coming in my room and getting in the bed with me because he was afraid to sleep alone. What was Khalid feeling? Was he feeling abandoned? I could not stop crying.

Everyday was monotonous. Tuesday could have been Friday. Friday could have been Wednesday. The days were all the same until Saturday. I awakened, cleaned the apartment, and made chicken salad sandwiches. Andreas went to the grocery store for lemons, so I could make fresh lemonade and to give Aunt Mary, Khalid, Grandma and me some time alone.

I opened the door on the first knock. Khalid ran into my arms and hugged me so tight that I almost could not breathe. I was equally happy to see him. Aunt Mary hugged me too. Grandma simply came inside of the apartment; she didn't greet me. She walked in and looked around the apartment.

77

"This is nice." I thanked her. We sat down while Khalid played with one of Andreas' video games.

"You really got yourself in a fine mess Thandie, but I'll tell you like I told that boy."

"His name is Andreas." I knew Grandma was going to blow this moment. I really didn't need to hear her degrade Andreas.

"Whatever, I ain't taking care of a baby. I've done the best I could for you, but I be damn if I take care of a baby. You grown enough to spread 'em you better be grown enough to take care of it." I could see tears in Grandma's eyes. I knew she was hurting. I didn't get an attitude with her or give her any rebuttal. I sat quietly and listened to her.

"Come on now Thelma," Aunt Mary intervened. "She's a child. She made a mistake; you don't have to be so hard." I wanted to cry but it was something about Grandma standing in my new home that I was now sharing with my man that made me feel I had to be strong and act like a woman.

"Is anyone hungry? I made chicken salad sandwiches."

"Did you cook the chicken with that lemon stuff?" Aunt Mary loved my chicken salad. I used lemon pepper and fresh grated lemon peels to season the chicken.

"Lemon pepper? Yeah, Aunt Mary, I know that's how you like it, so I made it with lemon pepper especially for you." We sat at the table talking. To my surprise, Grandma agreed to allow Khalid to spend alternate weekends with me. Before leaving, Grandma gave me an envelope with five hundred dollars.

"I'll send your check when it comes." I was still receiving a death benefit check from social security. "I'm sure you won't be going to college. So you'll have to wait until your 20th birthday before getting the rest of your money. Now take my advice, don't tell that boy all of your business. A woman needs to have something put away for hard times."

180⁰
One Hundred and Eighty Degrees

I love Thandisha. I have never met anyone who made me feel this good. She makes me feel like a man or the way I think that a man should feel. I don't know many men. Most of the men where I am from have been beaten down for so long by this system all they can do is move in with lonely women who can provide guaranteed, government shelter. Thandisha makes me feel strong. She makes me feel like I can accomplish anything. She is pure and untouched. She was a virgin when we met. I feel so special to have been the first man and prayerfully the only man who has touched her. I am going to be a good provider for my baby, and I am going to take good care of my woman.

My mentor has always said that no matter what the system has in store for me, I can be a man. He advised me that being a good, black man is cherishing a good, black woman, and no matter what obstacles come my way, I must never abandon my offspring. His advice was that I must fight for my children to the end. My mentor always said that a man's life is in vain if he is not a father to his children. I intended to be the best daddy in the world to my baby.

Thandisha was a hard nut to crack. I knew she was a good girl. Unlike the last time when I thought I was a father, I knew this baby was mine. I can't really explain Thandisha; I knew her mother was killed. This is why she and her brother

79

lived with their grandmother; but when I really think about it, I really don't know her. It's like she is holding something back. I know she is an excellent artist and a great cook. I know she still has nightmares about her mother. There is something about her eyes. Even when she is smiling, her eyes still look sad. It's a deep sadness.

Thandisha is what we call a cookie in the hood, a sweet girl. You never see her at any of the parties. She didn't have a typical teenage style. She had a style of her own. She was sexy as hell and gorgeous. Her beauty was so subtle that you could almost miss it. I think she does this on purpose. It's almost as if she doesn't want to be seen.

I told momma that I was going to be a daddy. She advised me to be careful. It was easy telling momma. I knew she wouldn't trip. I understood Thandisha's grandmother's anger. She had high expectations for Thandisha. She wanted more for her. It's not that my mother didn't have high expectations for me, just different expectations. When you have lived in the projects all of your life, it's different. My mother was okay as long as I was not using or selling drugs.

"Andreas, baby you know what happened before when you thought you were going to be a daddy." She was talking about Latanya. Yeah that did hurt, but I am over that.

"Momma, I know, but I have no doubt this baby is mine." I still feel special, she chose me. I still have the teeth marks on my shoulder from the first time we made love.

It is a major adjustment living with her. She wakes up every morning before sunrise without an alarm clock. She showers and spruces herself up and then she cleans the apartment. She never allows me to see her unkempt. She makes elegant meals including breakfast. I'm just a regular bacon and eggs kind of man, but she has brought an element of elegance to my life.

This pregnancy thing has been a trip. The bigger she gets, the more I want her, but she has lost almost total interest in sex. She gives it to me once a week. I think out of obligation, but when I get it, I am so damn happy. Sometimes I wish I could be the baby all tightly snuggled inside of her.

She is always complaining that she is tired. I understand why she is always so tired. She is six months pregnant and still awakens before sunrise and sits on the patio painting, or she may drink hot tea while reading the newspaper. Even with all of these idiosyncrasies, I love her. Although I am sure my life is going to change dramatically, I couldn't ask for anything better. I am truly grateful to God she chose me. Even though I have to get up sometimes in the middle of the night, go to the store to get strawberries and whipped cream, and this is after calling home asking if she needed anything before I leave work to come home, I feel as if I am the luckiest person on earth. I am truly on my way to becoming a man.

Khalid comes over every other weekend. I knew I wasn't getting any when he visits. I really didn't mind because she loved her brother. They had an attachment that would make an average man feel a little jealousy. Thandisha acted as if she was his mother and at the same time his best friend. She was very catering to her brother. He gave her respect I have never seen in a typical sibling relationship. When Khalid visited, the apartment was crowded. I really had to get on the ball and look for a bigger place.

I have gone to all of her doctor visits. I was so excited when I saw the baby during her first ultrasound. Though I could not see the detail that Thandisha claimed she saw, the shadowy outline brought tears to my eyes. Thandisha claimed she could see full detail. She and the nurse pointed at different features; all I could see was a roundish moving blob.

Thandisha will graduate in another three weeks. The classroom setting had become too stressful for her, so she completed her requirements in the Outbound Program for Pregnant Teens. I am very proud of her. It's been very hard for her. She lost her best friend, Ayanna. Ayanna quickly cut ties with Thandisha when she learned that she was pregnant. She tried to keep the pregnancy a secret from Ayanna as long as she could. When it became obvious she was pregnant, their friendship was over. Every time Thandisha called Ayanna, Ayanna was always busy or on the other line. It took Thandisha a while to get the message. I understand her pain from losing Ayanna. After all, they were best friends for years. I really didn't care for her; I found Ayanna bossy and overbearing, but she was Thandisha's best friend. I encouraged her to find other friends, but she basically stayed in the house cooking and painting.

I became anxious searching for a larger place, as that big moment was fast approaching. It was hard trying to find a place that satisfied Thandisha. She liked the West End area. We would look at places, but she didn't want it if it didn't have hardwood floors. If it had hardwood floors, then something would be wrong with the ceiling. She didn't realize that we had to take price into consideration. It made no sense to pay a grand a month for rent; I wanted to save money so that we could buy a home. She was totally clueless about money and had no concept of saving money.

When she got her social security check, I asked her to save something. I paid all of the bills and bought all of the groceries, but she didn't want to save. I put her name on my savings account and had to drag her down to the bank and literally take $200.00 from her monthly check. She wouldn't speak to me for a couple of days afterwards. And then she would spend the remaining $300.00 in a week. She would buy art supplies and clothes that she couldn't wear because she was too big and then get depressed because she couldn't wear them. But I noticed she rarely bought the baby anything.

It was the beginning of summer, the peak season for lawn care. I had saved $13,000 dollars. Not a lot of money for three years of working two jobs, but I was proud. Very proud because I know where I came from. I have a good momma, but she barely made the ends meet. I wanted to give my woman and baby all of the things I dreamed of having when I was a child like a spacious home with pretty, clean, new furniture and soft, thick, clean carpet. I accepted the hardwood floors because that's what Thandisha likes, but I really liked carpet. I walked on tile covered with a throw rug here and there all of my life. They do not allow wall to wall carpet in the projects.

I finally found an apartment we both agreed on. It was a two bedroom duplex in the West End. Although Thandisha didn't like the ceilings, she was okay with the apartment because she loved the hardwood floors. The bedrooms were humongous. Thandisha loves antiques, and the pieces that she has collected fit perfectly in the new apartment. Her decorative taste reminded me of women in the home decorating magazines.

I loved her so much. I was very proud of her too. I really wanted to give her my best. I wanted to take care of her. I mean really take care of her the way I would have wanted my pops to take care of momma. Momma had to worry about too many basic things while raising me and my siblings, and it took a toll on her.

Al, my cousin, helped me move into our new apartment. What should have taken all of three hours, took all damn day. Al and I moved the same piece of furniture about five times before she was satisfied.

I was in the living room hanging pictures when I heard Thandisha scream. I ran into the bedroom and found her kneeling forward holding her stomach. The front of her pants was soaked. She looked down at the wet spot on her pants, then looked up at me, and started crying.

"I peed on myself."

83

"No you didn't baby; your water broke. We're ready to have the baby." I hugged her so tightly that I could feel the wetness on my thighs.

"Oh God it hurts!"   She was bending forward and holding the lower half of her stomach. I was trying to remain calm. I am only a man. When I saw her grabbing her stomach and her face contorted in pain, I began to panic.   I called the doctor; he advised me to bring her to the hospital when the contractions were five minutes apart. I could not sit still listening to her scream, and I was too damn anxious to sit and time contractions. I grabbed her bag and proceeded to the door.

"Come on baby; let's go."

"Where are we going?

"To the hospital."

"I can't go like this." She looked down at the big wet spot in the front of her pants.

"Thandisha, sit down." I walked her over to the chair by the door. I pulled her pants down; her panties were soaked. I went to the bathroom, got a wash towel, and wiped her off.

"Oh God hurry, it hurts! It hurts!" She was crying still holding her stomach.   I pulled her top over her head and replaced it with a thin pullover dress.

"Come on; let's go."

"What about underwear?"

"Damn, you're getting ready to have a baby; you don't need any."

"I can't go without underwear." She screamed again. I looked in the boxes and found a pair of her underwear. She stepped in them, and I pulled them up to her stomach. The contractions were about eight minutes apart; I think. When we got to the emergency room, I called her grandmother. Ms. Thelma advised me to call her after the baby was born. I thought this was kind of cold; but she said that she was coming.

The doctors were getting on my nerves. They were taking their time and acting as if this was not an emergency. Thandisha was screaming so loud that I wanted to leave. I mean literally run out of the door. The nurse finally came in and checked her.

"You're not quite ready sweetie."

"What do you mean she's not ready? Don't you see that she is in pain?" I was perspiring profusely as if I were the one in labor getting ready to push a baby out.

"Well Sir, you don't want her to rupture her uterus do you?" I didn't know what she was talking about. I just wanted to stop my baby from hurting. I held her hand, as she tried to do the breathing exercises. She would start off breathing exactly like the video instructed but then she would end up screaming and cursing me out.

"Look what you did! Damn you!"

"Just breathe baby just breathe. Don't push yet. You're almost ready." She screamed out loud again calling her mother and father. I never knew she had a father. Well I knew she had a father, but I assumed he wasn't in her life that maybe she didn't know him.

The nurse came back in the room and checked her cervix again. "Sir/Ma'am, I think we're ready for this baby."

"You're ready baby." I changed into doc wear and went to watch my baby enter the world. They wheeled her into the delivery room. I stood at the top, but I could see. I held her up to push. She pushed hard. Her face was covered with tiny beads of perspiration.

"Push," I lifted her back up like I learned from the video taped birthing classes. Her face was tight; her veins protruded from her face. She pushed hard. I could see the baby's head. I stood amazed, as I watched my baby enter the world. Dr. Martin gave the command to push again. I was so mesmerized; I forgot to lift her up. Thandisha pushed again at the doctor's command.

I could see the baby's shoulders.   The next push, the baby entered the world.

"It's a girl." Dr. Martin suctioned her nose and mouth. She let out a loud wail.   He gave the baby to the nurse who passed her on to me.   I was amazed; I wanted to cry.   She was beautiful.   I knew I would do whatever I needed to do to take care of my baby.   I washed the baby and carried her to her mother.   She lifted her head and met my mouth with a long, passionate kiss.

The nurse took the baby to the nursery while Thandisha rested.   I called her grandmother; she said that she would come in the morning.   She was cold, but nothing could take away my joy today.   All of my family was at the hospital.   My brothers, sisters, aunts, uncles and cousins filled the waiting area. Thandisha appeared overwhelmed by all of my relatives.

"Boy, that's a pretty baby.   She gone have good hair just like her mother.   When they bald as an eagle that's how it turns out." My Aunt Annie was so into "pretty hair" that she only mated with men that could produce light-skinned children with wavy hair.   I thought this was strange because she was black as midnight with tight, course hair.   She passed this self-hate to her children.   All of her children married Caucasians, Mexicans, or Puerto Ricans.

I placed the baby's bed in our room.   I had everything in order when I brought my family home.   Thandisha was still sore from the stitches, so my mother stayed with us for two weeks. Thandisha was just there.   She really didn't relate to my mother. I was accustomed to everyone trying to create a good bond with my mother, as she has a very welcoming spirit.   My mother tried talking to her, but Thandisha's conversation consisted of providing answers to my mother's questions.   She did not initiate conversation nor did she sustain conversation with my mother.   I could tell she was uncomfortable, but I knew eventually they would get along.   Everyone likes my mother.

It took a month for Thandisha to start getting around normally. She lost all of the weight. Her stomach was flat as a pancake. She looked good. I came home today before going to the second gig expecting to get some. Thandisha was on the pill and was more in the mood these days. I was pissed off when I saw Jazmyne lying on the floor. Jazmyne is my sister who I truly love, but I honestly did not want Thandisha hanging out with her. I had stopped fighting Keekee, her boyfriend. I had my own family now and couldn't afford the trouble, and Jazmyne was trouble.

I know people try to blame the parents, but I can tell you my mother is not the blame for my trifling sister. I have five sisters and two brothers. We all worked our way out of the projects, but Jazmyne never understood that nothing is free; everything has a price tag. My mother did everything she could.

I have a lot of siblings. But no one can call my momma a whore. We all have the same father. When my daddy left us, my momma did not have skills to support us, so we had to live in the projects. Momma always told us that we made our own futures. She would often say, "We may live in the projects, but the projects are not in us." We didn't have money. My mother never owned a car, but once a month when her welfare check came, we would get on the train and travel to the upscale parts of town to see how other people lived.

My mother was very structured. After school, we immediately completed our homework. She would sit at the table with us and look over our homework. She was so good that I didn't' realize she could not read until I was almost out of junior high school. Dinner was always ready when we got home from school, and we ate a good, hot breakfast every morning.

Unlike most of the kids in the neighborhood, we were not allowed to go outside to play everyday. Sometimes we had to sit still, but Jazmyne was never satisfied. She had to have name brand clothes and shoes. She wasn't bold enough to steal them, so she dated older men who bought her things. My momma did not look the other way. She beat her and punished her, but none of this did any good. Jazmyne is Jazmyne, and she does what she wants to do.

Jazmyne had lost a lot of weight and looked tired. She and Keekee have their own place now, so I wondered why she was here. Thandisha was lying down with Kyia on her stomach. I hated when she held the baby lying down; it looked unsafe. What if she accidentally rolled over on the baby or allowed her to fall? Her hormones were still unstable, so I didn't say anything.

I went into the bathroom and showered. When I came out, she was awake and arranging her perfumes on the dresser. I walked behind her and wrapped my arms around her waist then slid my hand inside of her panties and massaged her hardened clit.

"Did I tell you I love you today?"

"No," she turned around. "I don't think you did." I kissed her. We closed the door. I enjoyed making love with Thandisha. She was very passionate.

"You took the pill today?" I hated to interrupt the mood, but as much as I loved Kyia, I was not ready to have another baby.

"Hell yeah, I don't ever want to go through that shit again." I hate when she curses; it just didn't sound right maybe for someone else but not Thandisha.

I was sitting on the bed watching her undress admiring the fullness of her breasts and the curve of her behind. She came over to the bed, straddled me and placed a passionate, moist kiss on my lips. I used my tongue to part her lips and explored her warm mouth. I slid down and lay flat on my back. She crawled up and planted her neatly shaven mound on my mouth. I open her lips and found the brown berry that always brought her pleasure. I licked and sucked. She rocked back and forth to the rhythm of my tongue. The wimpers and moans followed by pleas for me not to stop were music to my ears. I lifted her hips and slid her down to my throbbing rod. She wasn't ready. She took my rod in her hand, stroked it, and placed it in her mouth. She sucked and pulled until I was ready to explode. I moved her head she crawled back up, straddled me and place my erect manhood inside. She rocked back and forth; bounced up and down until she had an orgasm. I could look in her face and tell; her eyes were tightly closed and her mouth slightly opened. She collapsed on my stomach still shaking as if she were having a mild seizure. I rolled her on her back and went to work. Her body felt so damn good. Every time was always like the first time, good. I grabbed her legs and placed them around my shoulders. I was giving it to her deep and hard knocking the headboard against the wall. It was so damn good that I was almost screaming. She placed her hand over my mouth to muffle the sound, so Jazmyne would not hear. After I climaxed, I lay quietly holding her in deep thought. I have never known her to go for what she wanted like this before. Usually I am the one who initiates and sets the tone to our lovemaking. I met her eyes with a wide smile then quickly got up, took a quick shower, and got ready for work.

"Are you going to your second job today?"

"Of course, I have three mouths to feed."

"Andreas come on, you work too much; we never have fun anymore." She looked sad and disappointed.

"Baby, I'm trying to put something together for us. It won't be long." I kissed her and left. I passed Jazmyne who was now asleep on the sofa. I woke her up and told her to put a sheet on the sofa. I didn't like her with Thandisha and the baby.

Thandisha was 18 and didn't have a license, but she knew how to drive. She wanted to get a job. She would have been okay driving without a license, but that was too risky. I have seen too many brothers and sisters take small risk and end up in big trouble. I insisted that she get her license and drive legally.

Her social security check ends next month; she really needed to start selling her art instead of working a job. She had painted three beautiful pictures since having Kyia, but she wanted to find a job. I tried to explain to her that she should work for herself, so Kyia would not have to go to daycare. I wasn't ready for Kyia to start day care. I tried to convince her to sell her art at private showings. But she complained daily about being in the house with Kyia. My mother volunteered to keep Kyia, as she agreed with me that she was too young for daycare. Thandisha found a part- time job working from 8:00 am until noon at the library. I paid momma $50.00 per week to keep Kyia. I practically had to shove it down her throat to make her take it.

The job brought on more arguments. I filled the car with gas every Sunday night. I gave her lunch money. The problem was not what I did for her; the problem was that she didn't like to save. She cashed her check on Friday, and she was broke by Monday. She did buy diapers for the baby, and she bought an outfit every week for herself and Kyia. She and Kyia had so many clothes; it was pathetic. I had planed on quitting the night job; but then decided if we were going to buy a house, I had best continue working. I could not depend on Thandisha to help with anything financial. Nor could I depend on her as a partner in purchasing a home for our family. Her response was always, "*Whatever you want.*"

Although my business was doing well, I was still afraid to let the job go. I was afraid of not having enough money to provide for my family. I guess that's one of the effects of growing up poor; there is always the fear that you won't have enough.

Thandisha constantly complained about working and then keeping Kyia everyday. I had to remind her that I suggested she find friends so she could have a social life. She had not had another friend since Ayanna. Jazymne cannot be considered a friend. I hoped that she would end her relationship with my sister. I love my sister, but she is manipulative and untrustworthy. I am not exactly a people person, but I interact with my customers and co-workers at the plant. Momma agreed to keep Kyia until 8:00 p.m. on Fridays to give Thandisha time to herself. I was truly okay with this arrangement because I felt that she should get out more.

I was focused on my work when I heard my name on the intercom. I had an emergency phone call. The boss came and got me off the floor; it was momma. I panicked because she has never called me on the job. She was worried; it was 10:30 and Thandisha hadn't come for the baby. She said Kyia had a fever and was very irritable. Momma tried to take her to the emergency room, but they wouldn't see Kyia because she wasn't a parent or legal guardian. I panicked. My first instinct was Thandisha had an accident with the car. I clocked out and went to momma's to get Kyia so that I could take her to the emergency room. When I got there, Thandisha still had not come for Kyia nor had she called.

By the time Kyia and I reached the hospital emergency room, her temperature had climbed to 104. She was immediately given liquids and antibiotics. Momma was right; she had a bad ear infection. We stayed at the hospital until her temperature stabilized. While I waited, I called around to several hospitals to see if she was admitted. There was no Thandisha Riley Glaze checked in at any hospital in Atlanta, Georgia. We sat at the hospital for more than three hours. Thandisha did not page me nor had anyone heard from her.

When I got home, I called momma. She still had not heard from Thandisha. I thanked her for calling me when Kyia was ill and let her know that everything was okay.

Every time I attempted to place her in her crib, Kyia would scream. So I waited until she was sound to sleep before attempting to put her to bed. I was awakened around 3:00 am.

Thandisha was trying to get her key in the door. I sat up on the sofa, as she opened the door.

"Hey!" She jumped. I guess she was surprised I was awake. Jazmyne was with her. I asked Jazmyne to leave.

"Bro I need to spend the night; Keekee gone kill me." She walked through the door assuming it was okay for her to stay.

"Sounds personal sis."

"Come on now bro Keekee gone beat the hell out of me. Look at the time."

"Well you obviously like it. Go Jazmyne. Get out!" I opened the door and pushed her out of it. I looked at Thandisha who was standing by the door. She looked anxious. Her hair was loosely curled, thick, and beautiful. I could tell she had been to the hair salon. She looked sexy as hell. She was wearing a black dress that draped her thin, shapely body. I was turned on but too pissed off to touch her.

"Where in the hell have you been?"

"I was out with Jazmyne."

"Until 3:00 in the fucking morning? Doing what?"

"We were just hanging out." She had the nerve to act as if my asking questions were getting on her nerves.

"What about Kyia? Did you know I had to take her to the emergency room?" Her nonchalant attitude made me furious. We yelled and argued until we woke the baby. She went in the bedroom to get the baby. I followed her, and before she could reach to get Kyia, I pushed her out of the way. She tripped and landed on the floor. I picked up the baby, went in the living room, and watched television.

I heard water running in the bathtub, which made me suspicious. My mind took me places that I really didn't need to go. She stayed in the bathroom a long time. When she came out, I was in bed. She let the towel fall, put on one of my t-shirts, and came to bed. I was mad as hell, but I had a hard on out of this world; plus I wanted to make sure she wasn't fucking around.

She wrapped her arm around my waist. My back was turned to her. She slowly slid her hand across my side and then down to my manhood. That's all it took. I turned over. "Oh Andreas baby I'm sorry. I'm so sorry baby." She covered my face with passionate kisses. I didn't return the passion; I just wanted a good nut. She was on top of me holding on to the headboard giving it to me like she really wanted to cum. I was pushing it to her strong and hard. I relished the disappointment on her face when I climaxed. She didn't say anything. She fell on my stomach, rolled over, and went to sleep.

The next morning I left early. Thandisha and Kyia were sound to sleep. I had to cut ten yards; thank God I was finally able to purchase quality, landscape equipment. I had a good commercial lawn mower that could cut a two-acre yard in less than thirty minutes. I love doing lawn work. It's almost like play time for me. The smell of fresh, cut grass almost gets me high, and I get a lot of satisfaction out of planting and seeing the seeds grow. It's amazing how a seed grows into a little stump of greenery and then into a beautiful flower. Landscaping was like therapy for me. I was feeling so good that I let that shit Thandisha did yesterday roll off my back.

I finished early. When I came home, the car was gone. I figured she and Kyia were at the mall, Thandisha's favorite hang out. I sat down and watched television. My body was tired. Just as I dozed off, I heard the baby cry. At first, I thought I was dreaming surely she didn't. I knew that she wouldn't. I went into the bedroom. Kyia was standing in her crib in a diaper soaked with urine and feces. It took a second before I could pick her up. I could not move. Kyia and I stood still looking at one another. Finally, I took her out of the bed, removed the dirty diaper, bathed her, and powdered her down. I clung to her then fed her fruit before giving her a bottle.

I played with her for over an hour before Thandisha walked in the door. I placed Kyia in her walker. Thandisha stood still looking as if she were deciding whether or not to come inside. I grabbed her and pulled her inside of the apartment. I don't know what came over me, but I followed my first instinct. I slapped her so hard that a stinging sensation vibrated from my hand up to my shoulder. I totally lost control. I knew that I was hitting her with a closed fist, but I couldn't stop myself. I heard a mixture of crying from Kyia and screaming from Thandisha. When I pulled myself together, she was covering her face trying to block the blows. I couldn't believe it. I couldn't believe I was doing this. I had seen my father hit my mother more times than I care to remember. I vowed I would never hit a woman no matter what. I looked at Thandisha cowering on the floor. Part of me wanted to say I was sorry and beg her forgiveness. The other part of me wanted to kick her ass again and then throw her out in the street.

I went to my daughter and took her in the bedroom and held her. I held her so close that it seemed that our heartbeats were synchronized. I was confused. I knew I was doing what I was supposed to do. I was trying hard to be a man. I had nothing but my imagination as well as the advice of my mentor to guide me into manhood, but I was determined I was going to be a good man. I felt remorseful and anger towards Thandisha at the same time. I was ashamed. I still can't believe I actually hit her. I vowed to myself that I would leave her before I allowed myself to go this low with her again.

I went all kind of places in my head. I started noticing strange things like she stopped getting her brother every other week. She never had money although she was not buying anything for herself or the baby anymore. And worst of all she was hanging out with my sister.

Maybe she found someone and didn't know how to leave or how to tell me. This shit was getting wicked. I could not have imagined in my wildest dreams she would behave this way. Kyia and I left the apartment to visit my mentor. I had to get out of the apartment. I felt so many different emotions that I was suffocating. I told him that I hit Thandisha. I told him that I lost control when I came home and found the baby alone. He advised me to never hit her again but leave first. That positive, therapeutic, mentor shit sounded good, but damn, did he realize that my baby was left home alone? I don't even know how long she was alone. Kyia and I stayed away from the apartment for several hours.

When we returned home, I saw cigarette butts in the ashtray and smelled smoke. Thandisha was asleep on the sofa. I hated cigarette smoke, and she knew that I would never allow anyone to smoke in the house. What would make her want to smoke anyway?

I didn't wake her. I could see her eye was swollen. She had on a t-shirt and underwear. She was bruised pretty badly. I didn't want to wake her because I really didn't want to face her. I didn't want to see her; regardless of what she had done, I had no right to hit her.

I took Kyia with me to rent movies. She was asleep, but I woke her up. I didn't trust leaving her in the house alone with her mother. When we got back, Thandisha was awake. She had taken a shower; I could tell because her hair was wet and stuck to her head. Her face was swollen. Her eyes were puffy and developing a black ring around them. I put Kyia on the floor. She immediately crawled to her mother. Thandisha picked her up and held her. I really didn't want her to touch Kyia, but she was still her mother.

"I bought Chinese take out. You want some?"

"Yeah thanks." I really didn't want to give her ass nothing, but that would have been a little too rude not to mention somewhat immature. I brought two plates and two sodas in the living room. I prepared her plate while she played with Kyia. We ate the Chinese food and watched the movies in silence.

I was enjoying this moment until Jazmyne knocked on the door. She looked at Thandisha. "Damn gull you got a good ass kicking didn't you?" She laughed. Thandisha nor I felt the humor.

"I was wondering. Do you want to go to the 24 kt tonight?"

"Hell no, she don't want to go nowhere."

"No girl not tonight."

"Nor any other night." I pulled Jazmyne outside.

"Look don't come around here anymore. I don't know what's going on. You're my sister and I know you ain't nothing but trouble."

"You think you're so damn much. But you ain't no better than me. We come from the same damned sorry ass place. You ain't no damn better than the rest of us. She rolled her eyes and jerked her neck. I pushed her out of the door and slammed it in her face. We continued to watch our movies. Actually we were really just looking at the screen. I was waiting for her to say something, and she was doing the same.

"I'm sorry about today. I went to get something to eat and stopped by the store. I didn't think I would be gone that long."

"Thandisha, Kyia is a baby. You can never leave her alone. Don't you know this? She could choke; anything could happen." She was crying uncontrollably.

"I am so sorry." She was so different. Earlier it was as if she did not have emotions. She acted as if she was totally disconnected from her emotions.

"What's the matter with you baby? You been acting strange every since you been hanging with Jazmyne." She simply looked at me. She didn't say anything. Then I kind of felt guilty. She came over to me. I held her close. She cried; I mean really snotting. I wiped her face with one of Kyia's cloth diapers. She kissed me with a deep and yearning passion. Kyia was on the floor looking. She put her hands down my pants and slid down to give me head. I pulled her up.

"Come on, baby wait; Kyia is watching." Where was she getting this shit? I was confused, but I liked it. I gave Kyia her medicine and a bottle; she finally dozed off on the blanket.

I never worked on Sunday. Sunday was my day of rest; I was truly exhausted from working the job and running my business to go anywhere. Thandisha constantly complained that I needed to spend more time at home. She was right. I really did need to spend more time with my family, but I was consumed with making enough money. I wanted to have enough to provide security for my family. She was lying on the bed flipping channels. Even after the baby, she still looked good. A lot of women let themselves go after they have children and believe me I do understand. Taking care of a baby ain't no joke. But Thandisha still had it. She still put herself together very nicely. She was happy when I offered to take her and Kyia out for the day. We got dressed and went to Thandisha's grandmother's house.

I can't say that Ms. Thelma is a model grandmother. To be honest, she is a horrible grandmother. She has seen Kyia three times. Ms. Thelma fussed over Kyia. She tried to hold Kyia, but Kyia wasn't having it. She clung to me screaming every time Ms. Thelma tried to take her out of my arms. Ms. Thelma gave up and admired her while I held her.

"Thandisha was the same way. She didn't want to be bothered with anyone but her daddy." I found this strange; Thandisha never mentioned that she had a relationship with her father. She never talked about him; I have never seen pictures of her with her mother or her father. I assumed she was like many people I know who did not know their father, or the father was not part of their life.

I noticed Thandisha and Mrs. Thelma really did not have very much to say to one another. They greeted one another like distant friends unlike granddaughter and grandmother. It was strange; however, Thandisha was very responsive to Khalid. She made French Toast, Khalid's favorite. We ate while Ms. Thelma tried to get Kyia's attention. Kyia continued to ignore her.

Khalid wanted to go to the mall, and as usual, Thandisha obliged him. I had spent all of the cash. I never wrote checks except on Friday to pay myself and pay my help. I pulled over to the bank and used my ATM card to get money from my savings. I looked at the balance. It was short by $2300. I took the money and walked back to the car.

"I don't believe this shit."

"What?" I looked in my workbag and pulled out my account register.

"Something's wrong."

"What?" Thandisha was fixated on filing her nails. Although she was responsive, her eyes were glued to her nails.

"They have shortened me over two grand. You haven't taken any money out have you?" I could not see why she would need to. She worked everyday. Though it's only part time, she doesn't have to pay bills. She does not pay childcare, and sometimes I even give her lunch money.

"No. Why would I do that?" She looked as if I had insulted her. I felt guilty for asking.

"It must be a mistake with the bank. I will straighten it out on Monday."

Khalid wanted to go to an electronic store. He was fifteen, but not a street-smart fifteen. He still played video games. He was active in after school activities. The disturbing thing was that it seemed to me their Aunt Mary, who really wasn't an aunt, was his best friend. Thandisha says that she is the closest thing to a male role model that Khalid would ever have. I thought this strange. I mean he is fifteen years old, and she is an elderly woman. Why didn't he hang out with other fifteen year old guys in the neighborhood? I didn't understand what Khalid would have in common with an elderly woman. Khalid spent the entire $200 I withdrew from my account. It must be in their blood. He was like his sister. Neither of them understood the value of money.

On Monday morning, Thandisha awakened ill. I thought she may have gotten a stomach virus because she was sweating and constantly in the bathroom. We had eaten a lot of junk food yesterday while hanging out with Khalid. I didn't want to leave her, but I had six yards to cut. I called momma, but she didn't answer the phone. I reluctantly left Kyia with Thandisha and gave her instructions on Kyia's medicine schedule.

I drove to the storage building and loaded my equipment. I drove back to my old neighborhood to get Jerome, my helper; he was drunk as hell. I didn't feel like being bothered with him. I drove off, as he staggered towards the truck. It was 9:30 and still cool outside. It took me two hours to cut my first yard. I cut MRH's yard every two weeks. I was so proud of this yard that I would have serviced it for free.

When I first started my business, I had a walk behind lawn mower that I picked up and threw in the trunk of my car. MRH is a small manufacturing plant. John Murray owns it. I drove by one day and saw that the yard was getting out of hand and offered my services. Initially, Mr. Murray thought I was crazy when he saw my mower. He could not believe I would attempt to cut two acres with a cheap, walk behind, mower. He gave me the contract, and the rest is history. I went into the office and gave him my invoice. As usual, he came out of his office and talked with me about politics and the importance of investments. I really respected Mr. Murray, and he respected me. Through him, I had gotten four other commercial accounts. He was a good businessman; what really impressed me most is that he took good care of his family. It seemed that the Mrs. was always going on vacation or expensive shopping sprees.

Initially, Mr. Murray intimidated me. He was no-nonsense and very straightforward, but he is one of the few white men that I have known who showed true friendship. It's just like my mentor has always told me, "If you conduct yourself like a man then you will be respected as a man by any man no matter if he is black, white, or green."

"How's the baby?"

"Mr. Murray, she is getting so big. She's wonderful."

"Well when are you going to bring her by the office, so I can meet Ms. Wonderful?"

"Real soon I've been so busy; I haven't had time. I promise; I will bring her."

"My brother with the realty company mentioned how much he likes your work." He pulled out a piece of paper and gave me a phone number.

"When you get a chance, call him." We shook hands, and I left for the bank in hopes of straightening out the $2300 discrepancy.

As usual, the line was long. The line is never this long when I transact business in the predominately white neighborhoods. Luckily they did have a line for commercial accounts. I talked to one of the bank officers and asked for a print out of my account. I couldn't believe my eyes. Thandisha had taken over 2300 dollars within the last two months.

We were saving to buy a house. She did put money in the account but nothing equivalent to 2300 dollars. Besides, we agreed not to touch the money without telling each other. I was puzzled because she hadn't bought anything for herself or Kyia. What was she doing with the money? I was certain that it had to be another man. My mind went back to the night she came home and took a bath. I was about to really nut up but then decided to put this on hold. I had three more yards to service. Hell, no matter what was going on with Thandisha, I had to care of Kyia.

It was two o'clock when I went home. I was grateful for a break. The temperature can get painfully hot in Atlanta, Georgia. Today was one of those hot and humid days. I put my key in the door, but the safety latch hindered me from opening the door. I heard steps hustling around the apartment. "Thandisha, open the door!" She didn't come to the door. "Thandisha, open the fucking door." I gave her a few more seconds to open the door then I kicked it in breaking the safety latch.

The apartment was smoky, but not a cigarette smoke. It was a thin, cloudy and stubborn smoke that didn't move. It was not a marijuana smoke. But a subtle smoke that was kind of sweet but pungent at the same time. I walked in the living room; Keekee and Jazmyne looked crazy. Jazmyne had lost a lot of weight and looked like pure hell. I picked up the lamp and swung it at Keekee and pushed Jazmyne out of the door knocking her ass on the floor. Keekee left Jazmyne on the floor almost tripping over her running outside.

I went into the bedroom; Kyia was asleep with a bottle of cold medicine clumsily lying next to her. I felt as if I were trapped in a horrible nightmare. I walked back to the living room. She was sitting on the sofa; I stood behind her staring at the back of her head in total disbelief. I walked in front of her. Her face was an ashen, gray color, and she looked bad. There were no words to describe how bad she looked.

"Did you give her this?" She looked at the bottle of cold medicine and didn't say anything. She was acting kind of antsy but not nervous just antsy. Her not answering was an indication I was right; she had given Kyia the cold medicine.

"How much did you give her?"

"Not a lot, not even a full teaspoon." I walked out of the living room and back into our bedroom with the baby. I looked at Kyia again. She looked okay; she was drowsy. I was shocked and still in total disbelief. I didn't know how to deal with this. I placed Kyia back in her crib and went back in the living room with Thandisha.

"Why did you take the money?"

"What fucking money?" I looked at her. I couldn't say anything. I was surprised. She was bold as hell. I didn't know who the hell this was. The face and body were the same. But who or what occupied it was a stranger.

"I went to the bank; why did you take over 2300 dollars out in less than two months?"

"I didn't take your damn money!"

"Don't lie to me!"

"What the hell is wrong with you anyway?" I noticed that she was clinging to her purse. When I snatched it out her hand, she lunged at me like a wild animal. It was like she jumped off the sofa and into my chest without even putting her feet on the floor. I pushed her back on the sofa and opened the bag. When I saw it, I almost collapsed. I couldn't believe this. I was shocked; I couldn't control myself. My body shook uncontrollably. My heart fell. It was a lipstick top with a broken ballpoint pen burned into the side. The tube was covered with aluminum foil. It was still warm. Why in the hell would she have a crack pipe? I wanted to believe that it was Jazmyne's. My baby would never risk what we have for this, but no matter how hard I tried, I could no longer ignore the signs. I went into the bedroom and packed a bag for Kyia.

There were so many women in my neighborhood on that shit. I have seen it drag down some of the people I grew up with, many of whom were once honest, hard working and respectful people. It seems to drag women worse because when they run out of money, they can turn a trick for a hit. Not only does it fuck up the user, but it devastates the entire family. I didn't know what to do. I just knew that I had to get my baby away from this scene. She sat still with her knees tightly pulled against her chest. I couldn't tell if she was crying because she was hurting or crying because her secret had been revealed. I walked from the living room back to the bedroom about five times before I could say anything to her.

"Who gave this to you?" She didn't answer; her face was folded in her hands; she was crying. It was not a loud free flowing cry. It was the kind of cry where you don't want anyone to know, and you want to keep it to yourself. I pushed her head out of her hands.

"Did you hear me? Who gave you this?"

"I saw Jazmyne doing it, and I tried it."

"How long? How long have you been doing this?"

"About six months."

"Six fucking months! How? How could I not have known? Give me the keys to the fucking car!" She didn't move, so I snatched open the purse again, threw the pipe on the floor, and crushed it with my foot

"No! No!" She was crying and screaming at the same time. She was on her knees trying to put the pipe back together. I knocked it out of her hand and pushed her away from it. I went through her purse and took the car keys. I went back in the bedroom and grabbed Kyia, changed her diaper, and left.

"Where are you going with Kyia?" She was crying uncontrollably; I could barely understand what she said.

"You need to decide what you are going to do by the time I get back. You can either get some help or get out. I mean it!" God knows I didn't want her to leave. I loved her so much. I didn't want Kyia to have the life I had. I wanted her to have her mother and her father in the same home. I didn't want Kyia to ever question the love of either of her parents.

I drove around for two hours trying to decide if I wanted to go to my mother's house. I really didn't want to burden her. But I could not think of anywhere else to go.

The screen door was latched, but the wooden door was open. She came to the door and unlatched the screen, and held it

open for Kyia and me. I stepped inside and stood in the middle
of the living room with a blank stare. I looked at her and broke
down.

"Andreas, what's wrong?" I couldn't talk.   "Arnell,
come and get the baby!" She took Kyia from my arms and called
for my sister.

I sat on the sofa crying for what seemed like an eternity.

"Baby, tell momma what's wrong." She placed my head
on her chest like she used to when I was ten years old and rocked
me back and forth.

"Momma, she's on drugs. She's using crack."

"Who? Who's on drugs baby?"

"Thandisha."

"Thandisha?" She appeared shocked. Arnell came back
in the living room obviously eavesdropping. Kyia reached for
me trying to wiggle out of her arms.

"What's wrong?" Momma waited for me to say it again.
She was very respectful of our individual privacy.

"Thandisha is smoking that shit. She is on crack." Arnell
didn't look surprised.

"I told you momma; you know Jazmyne is on that shit
too.   And since they are together all of the time, I knew
Thandisha had to be doing it too.   Tell him momma that's why
you won't allow Jazmyne in the house."

"Why didn't someone tell me?" Momma held her head
down.

"I had to give Jazmyne to the Lord. I just couldn't
continue seeing her so messed up or hear about all of those dirty
things she was doing." Momma was crying so uncontrollably
that I could barely understand her. "Lord knows I did the best I
could. If I didn't do right it was because I didn't know."

"What am I suppose to do momma?" I hoped that she
would have a magic answer. I wanted something definite from
her, something tangible that would work for sure like when I was

a child, and I was afraid of the boogey man and she would come into the room and turn on all of the lights in my room, and we would look under the bed and in the closet and see that nothing was there and then I could go back to sleep.

"Pray and give it to the good Lord. Take care of yourself and my grandbaby." I thought to myself. Is that all? Surely she would have a more tangible suggestion than this.

"But I love her momma."

"I love Jazmyne too, but I did all I could then gave it to God. Son, you are a hard worker. You are doing a good job. You have come a long way. Don't stop now; take care of yourself first and everything will fall into place." I stopped crying, but I was still in pain. At that moment, the concept of powerlessness was very real to me. I would have done anything to erase this shit. We sat for a while not saying anything.

"All of this crying is making me hungry. Want some dinner?" We went into the kitchen. Momma cooked Sunday dinner Monday through Friday and not that canned stuff either. She cooked fresh greens, candy yams, ham and corn bread. I sat at the table, as she prepared my plate with man size portions of everything. She took Kyia from my arms and sat her on her knee. She then smashed up corn bread with the greens and fed it to her.

"Momma, I have baby food. I don't think she supposed to be eating that yet."

"You ate it; look at you." Kyia gobbled it down barely swallowing one mouthful before opening her mouth for more.

"Momma, I have to go back to work. I don't want to take Kyia..."

"Don't you even ask boy. You know I will watch my grandbaby anytime."

I left Kyia with momma and went to finish the rest of my lawns. There was no way that I could make it to my second job tonight. I was drained not physically but emotionally. I called in and took the night off. I knew momma would have kept Kyia, but there was no way I could have worked. Besides Kyia was not momma's responsibility; she was my responsibility.

I went home for a quick break before cutting the last yard; Thandisha was sitting on the sofa. She couldn't look at me. I really didn't have anything to say to her. We cordially greeted one another. She was dressed in baggy jeans and a t-shirt.

"Where's Kyia?"

"I took her to my mother's."

"Why did you do that?" I could not believe the nerve of this woman or whatever this was. How could she ask a question like this?

"Because I have more lawns to cut. Oh you didn't think I would leave her with you did you?"

"Why not? I am her mother." I wanted to slap her ass around again, but it wasn't worth the guilt I knew I would feel later.

"Yeah you are her mother, but a sorry ass excuse for one."

"I am not a bad parent."

"You're an awful parent. You left her in the house alone. You allowed drugs to be used in the house while she was here and to make sure she didn't interrupt your party, you gave her fucking cold medicine. I guess you want to make her a druggie too. And to top it all off, you're a damn thief."

"Fuck you Andreas!"

"Fuck you bitch!" I left on that note. I felt horrible for talking to her so harshly, but she was really getting under my skin. I had to get out and away from her before I hurt her. By the time I reached the car, I was filled with anger. I couldn't leave. I turned over the engine three times, but I could not manage to place the transmission in drive to leave. When I came back into the apartment, she was still sitting on the sofa. I walked over to her. She still did not move.

"What the hell did I do to deserve this from you? Is there anything you wanted that I didn't provide for you?" She didn't say anything. Her nonchalance was working my nerves. Without thinking, I grabbed her and pulled her off of the sofa. We were screaming at each other neither of us hearing what the other said. Then she said it, and I couldn't believe it.

"I had a mother and a father." She spoke like a confession as if she had done something wrong. She described her father as a very successful businessman, something that I was striving to become. She told me about That Day. *That Day when her father killed her mother.* She couldn't give details; though I was inquisitive, I knew that I should simply listen. She only said that she and Khalid were there. She said that she was a happy little girl and that she loved her mother, but she adored her father. She talked about Friday presents. She talked about the guilt she felt for still loving him. Guilt for still wanting to see him and anger for not knowing where he was. She was crying holding herself with her knees curled tightly to her chest. I was too angry to touch her. I tried but couldn't touch her.

"Please Andreas help me. Please don't leave me." I have seen Thandisha cry a few times, and it touched something so deep inside of me that it hurt. How could I help her? I was trying to build one man from several images. I had no example to follow only the advice of a mentor or a minister here and there or a boss that I wanted to emulate. She was still crying. I was powerless because I knew there was nothing that I could do, so I finally walked over and held her. She was wrapped in my arms and snuggled very close to me. I kissed her and tried to reassure her that everything would be okay. I didn't know how, but I knew that it would all be okay.

"I am going to quit the job at the plant and work my business. Maybe if I am home more often, it would take some pressure off of you." I took three days of vacation from work to spend with Thandisha. It turned out to be a good decision. I found that my body actually needed the rest. I had been working two jobs for so long that I almost forgot what it was to rest. We didn't leave the house the entire three days.

On Thursday morning, I got up, showered, and cut my scheduled lawns. When I came home, Thandisha was deep in sleep. I kissed her and left for the second gig at the plant. I spoke with Mr. Duncan before going to the work line. Without going into detail, I told him that I was having family problems and offered to give him a two-week notice.

"Son, I will accept your resignation; but I thought you were saving for a home for your family."

"Yes Mr. Duncan, that was definitely the plan, but something has kind of come up making that next to impossible right now."

"You have worked here for a while now. You're a damn good worker. There is a supervisor position coming open. Management has their eye on you. Why don't you just take some time off and work out whatever is going on? Don't quit now. You have your woman and a baby to think about."

"Yes sir I know. But to tell the truth my family is the reason I need to quit. My girl is having some problems, and she needs my support. If I get a home or promotion and she is not there, what's the point?" He didn't like my answer, but he did accept my resignation with a two-week notice. I was kind of relieved. I knew that I would eventually be able to purchase a home. It may take a little longer, but it will happen.

I went home; not knowing what to expect, so I didn't expect anything. She was in the bed lying on her stomach asleep. I went in the bathroom and took a shower. I was hungry; I went in the kitchen and warmed leftovers. I was laying on the sofa watching television when she came in the living room. I looked at her, greeted her, and continued to watch television.

"Where is Kyia?"

"She is with my mother. I'm tired. I let her stay with momma." She came over and lay on the sofa with me. Initially I didn't touch her. I was angry, scared and hurt. I thought I had everything a man could want. I had a beautiful baby; I made decent money. I thought Thandisha and I were solid, but this latest revelation has turned my world upside down, but I truly still love her. I eventually wrapped my arms around her. I held her very close to me. I held her so close that I could feel her heartbeat. I wanted to be godlike to her. I wanted to protect her and take all of her pain away. I wanted to make everything okay. I was tired. Thandisha was tired; we went to sleep.

When the alarm went off, I didn't want to get up. I was exhausted. Not a physical tired but a mental tired. She was cradled in my arms holding me tight. I tried to slide from under her, but she awakened anyway.

"Good morning," I placed a soft kiss in the center of her forehead.

"Good morning." We lay still in the bed holding one another.

"Are you hungry? Do you want me to cook breakfast before you go?"

"No that's okay; get some rest."

"Are you bringing Kyia home?"

"I don't know."

"What do you mean?" Surely she understands why I would not bring my baby home. Surely she knows that after this latest revelation, I would not trust her with Kyia alone.

"I have to work tonight." She knew not to say anything. I kissed her and showered. When I left, she had fallen asleep again on the sofa. Before closing the door, I reminded her that Jazmyne nor Keekee should come in the house. She didn't say anything, but I knew she got the message.

225^0
Two Hundred and Twenty Five Degrees

He thinks it is so easy. He doesn't understand. I am trying. I have not used crack for a while now. I am trying, but it is so hard. Even when I heard a knock on the door, I did not answer. I was afraid that it was Jazmyne or Keekee. I didn't want to get high. I was too afraid to start. Because once you get that first hit, it's over. Everything goes down hill from the first hit. I never intended for it to get like this. I never, in my wildest dreams, thought I would get hooked. I thought I could control it. But I couldn't. I would have never allowed it to get out of control if it were in my power. I fought hard for the control, but each time I was defeated. Each time I was defeated, I felt more and more like a loser. The more I felt like a loser the more I needed to use.

I cooked chicken manicotti smothered in marinara sauce and cleaned the apartment from top to bottom then started on a picture of Andreas and Kyia. I hoped he would bring her home tonight. I love my baby. But when I am smoking, it blocks everything. The only thing I can feel is the urge to use more drugs and fear I will run out. I wish like hell I never tried it. Sometimes just thinking about it, oh God even now when I am thinking about it, I get so anxious that I have to clear my bowels.

I saw Jazmyne smoke crack a while back. I didn't try it for a long time, but I remember the look on her face. She had gotten into a fight with Keekee. She was upset and crying. But after she inhaled the smoke from the pipe, the anger and hurt on her face was replaced by a peaceful, euphoric expression.

I tried it for the first time after Kyia was born. I was feeling a lot of pressure. My whole life had changed. Even though Andreas was with me and totally supported me, I still felt alone. He was gone all day and half of the night. On the outside, I looked okay. I dressed myself up, but even that was a copycat style of some chick I saw in a magazine. On the inside, I was empty and still haunted by the memory of That Day. It was as if my past was constantly stalking me.

I used crack to stop thinking about the memories. It allowed me to pretend I never had a mother or father as if that life never existed. I went several years with the memories of momma and daddy locked safely away from my conscious mind. But after I had Kyia, I couldn't stop thinking about them. I was constantly feeling the pain over and over again. I was always thinking about momma, remembering her smile, her look, and all of her unique facial expressions. I missed looking at her beautiful face. My fond and beautiful memories of my momma were replaced by a deep and empty longing to see her. I would have given anything just to touch her and daddy. I felt so much guilt for still loving him, longing to see him, and still thinking he could make everything okay. I could not think about momma and daddy and not think about That Day; the two went hand in hand. My own mind was attacking me; I declared war on myself. That's what happens when you use crack. You can't control the compulsive obsessive nature of the drug. Sometimes I wouldn't want to do it, but I couldn't help myself. I couldn't stop myself at will. Using made me feel okay; it allowed moments to escape the horrible, fixed images and thoughts that were constantly occupying space in my mind.

He thinks that it is so easy. Andreas has a foundation; he knows what he wants. I don't have a foundation. Grandma provided for my physical needs, but my emotional needs were totally neglected. We never talked about That Day. We never talked about momma or daddy. We really didn't live together; we lived amongst each other. There were so many times I wanted to write daddy. Even though he did what he did, he was the only parent I had left. I don't know how many years he was sentenced to prison. I don't even know what the actual charges were. Grandma may have known, but I knew better than to ask her.

Andreas is a good man. He is strong. He is a good father. But I had no purpose and was simply occupying space. I know God placed him in my life for a reason. It felt good having someone love me, but I really didn't love myself. I was too empty, so I couldn't reap the rewards of his love. The only thing I felt good about was my art and cooking. I put a lot of feeling into my art and a lot of love into my cooking, just like momma. When momma gave away her recipes, she would write down the ingredients and the last ingredient was always "two cups of love."

People loved my art. They loved my cooking, especially my pastries, so I put a lot of energy into them and became a great artist and a great cook. When I paint, I have total control. I can create my world any way I want with the stroke of a paintbrush, charcoal, or pencil. I had been painting all day. Well at least since Andreas left. I was tired of painting, so I made lunch and turned on the television. As usual, there was nothing on the television. I have never watched a lot of television anyway. When I was younger, momma rarely allowed Khalid and me to watch television; instead, we played games and read books. Television was a treat like going to the movies.

My life is so different now. I have been exposed to all kinds of people. Most of these people are not really people but demons that have taken on human form. The evil, sick behavior associated with drugs is a nightmare. It is worst than any boogey man that I could have ever imagined. It's like carrying the boogey man with you all of the time.

I knew I would never be the same. Evil has a way of changing you permanently. When I smoked, I would usually go to Terri's house. Jazmyne introduced me to Terri when I first started smoking crack. Terri lives in run down apartments owned by a run down slumlord. She has four children with three baby daddies. She doesn't work, but she does "favors" for people to keep her rent paid. We would sit in her apartment all day smoking and drinking. Even when her children came home from school, the party would continue. Her children would walk in and speak to her as if this was normal. She may place the pipe down to nonchalantly ask about homework and then quickly continue the party. I sometimes felt guilty for smoking crack when her children were home; however, my guilt did not stop me from continuing to smoke.

We would start off buying a gram. It would be gone in an hour. Terri never had money, but she would allow people to sit in her home to use, so she could smoke for free or she would allow drug dealers to set up camp in her apartment. Jazmyne never had money either, but she would steal from Keekee or turn tricks.

Addicts, the broke ones, play a trap game. It took me a while to get hip to it. Jazmyne would give me a small hit, and that's all it would take. Once I started, I couldn't stop. I would go to the bank and withdraw $200 at a time. I went through this vicious cycle all day sometimes. Andreas thought I was working. In fact, I only worked a few months, and when I did work, I spent my entire check in the crack house with Jazmyne. This is how I ended up spending over $2300 of Andreas' money. I didn't mean to do it. I was somewhat conscious of what I was doing. I knew Andreas was very meticulous about his money; his checking and savings account registers are balanced to the penny. He can even project his quarterly interest to the penny. I knew he would eventually find out I was taking money from the account, but my cravings were so strong that at the time, I didn't care about the consequences. I was only concerned with getting high.

Initially, I would share everything, but now it seems the drug is making me selfish to where it's all about me. I wanted it all to myself. I would usually smoke the last gram by myself, and everyone would get mad sometimes to the point they would want to fight. I was oblivious to the danger of getting high in the presence of drug craving addicts. As long as I had my rock, I really didn't give a damn about anything. I knew it was a use game, but I was getting something out of it. I didn't care. It was a crazy game.

For now, I still have some morals about myself. I do not sleep with dealers for it. Jazmyne once told me that she slept with D380 for a gram and tried to convince me to sleep with him too. D380 is a supplier to the street peddlers in Jazmyne's neighborhood. Sleeping with a supplier can bring celebrity status in this game. When I look as Jazmyne, I see myself if I don't stop. Right now I want one. I want one bad. Keekee, Jazmyne's boyfriend, is always propositioning me. He tells me to keep my money and rubs the inside of my palm when he places the rock in my hand. Andreas would kill me. I guess I would kill myself.

I heard Andreas place his key in the door, and Kyia's familiar whine. When he opened the door, I was standing in the threshold waiting to greet them. Kyia reached for me; I gladly took her out Andreas' arms.

"Does she need her diaper changed?" I checked. She was wet. Andreas went into the bathroom to shower. I cleaned the kitchen sink, so I could bathe Kyia without Andreas looking over my shoulder. I poured baby bath oil in the sink and allowed her playtime in the water. I washed her hair, dried her, and powdered her down. She felt so good. Her skin was smooth and soft. Andreas came back into the kitchen with his back still wet.

"Did you have a nice day?"

"Yeah," he was still acting kind of dry. I waited for him to say something about me bathing Kyia in the sink; he didn't.

"What about you?"

"I kept busy. I did a lot of cleaning."

"I see; everything looks nice."

"Are you hungry?"

"Yeah," he answered cold and nasty. I could tell he was trying to piss me off so that we could argue, but I was determined not to argue. I prepared him a plate filled with chicken manicotti and buttered garlic bread on the side and placed it on the table in front of him. It always amazed me how much Andreas eats and still managed to maintain his sleek physique. The food must have been good. He ate without saying a word. Everything was going good until he opened his mouth again.

"You okay? You didn't do any of that shit today did you?"

"No, I fought it; Jazmyne knocked on the door two times, but I didn't open it." He smiled; I was happy that he finally gave me a genuine smile. He has been so harsh.

"That's good. That's real good."

"My stomach has been cramping all day, but I made it."

He smiled easily this time.

"That's good baby; that's real good." Kyia was fussy. I gave her to her father while I washed dishes and warmed her bottle.

"Thandisha, you don't have to warm it; she is old enough to drink it cold. In fact, she is too old for a bottle any way. She is almost a year old." I hate when he does that. He acts as if he knows everything and as if I don't know anything. He seems to forget when he worked all day and night; I was the one who took care of her.

"Yeah I know, but it is better on her stomach if it's warmed. My mother gave me and Khalid warm milk until we were five years old." He didn't say anything.

I cradled Kyia in my arms, and gave her the warmed bottle. She looked deeply into my eyes. If not for myself then I have to stay clean for my daughter. I love my baby. It may seem as if I don't, but I do. I was tired. Andreas was reclined on the sofa with the remote flipping channels. His constant changing of the channels was aggravating. Kyia and I went to bed. I placed her down on the bed close to me. She was snuggled tightly in my arms.

"Thandisha, she is not supposed to sleep in our bed. She has her own bed." Before I could say anything, he took Kyia out of the bed and placed her in her crib. After placing Kyia in her crib, he walked over to his side of the bed and jumped in the bed. I can't say he was trying to disturb me on purpose, but it seemed to me that he could have gotten in bed much gentler. I bounced up and down at least three times before the mattress finally settled. When he reached for me, I didn't respond.

"I'm a little tired tonight." The truth was that I was angry and hurt. He acts as if I don't know anything. I messed up. I messed up bad, but I am not stupid. Kyia awakened as usual at 3:00 am. I changed her; before I could finish, he was checking to see what I was doing.

"What?" I rolled my eyes. He was acting as if he didn't understand. He makes me so fucking sick always acting as if he is so damn perfect.

"I am changing her diaper and getting her a bottle. Do you have to watch everything that I do?"

"Maybe I do."

"When she was born, I was here not you. I took care of her all day and night. So I messed up, but I am still her mother." I reached to get her. He pushed me out of the way. He picked her up, went in the kitchen, and gave her a cold bottle of milk.

He slept on the sofa with Kyia the rest of the night; I slept in the bed. Actually, I did not sleep. I lay still in the bed listening to music. At sunrise, I got out of bed and showered. It was cool outside. The air smelled good. I made an omelet and hot tea, sat on the patio, and read the newspaper. He walked into the living room and placed Kyia on the sofa. She was still asleep. I continued reading the paper. I figured he was going to shower and leave for work. I looked forward to him leaving, so I could spend time with Kyia alone. I was very uncomfortable with Kyia when Andreas was around. I feel as if I am under constant surveillance.

I was livid when he came back into the living room fully dressed with Kyia's bag in his hand. I knew he was taking her to his mother. We made eye contact. I didn't say anything neither did he. He left. I was angry and frustrated; I had no money or transportation. The walls were closing in on me. I didn't want to be home. I knew Jazmyne would come, and the way I felt, I probably would open the door. To keep my mind occupied, I cleaned a spotless kitchen, mopped a clean floor, and dusted dustless furniture.

I felt a sudden and almost urgent need to leave the house. I knew he had an extra car key. I went to the closet and checked the pockets of all of his clothes throwing each piece in a pile on the floor, as I finished. I could not find the car key. I pulled the backs out of all of the pictures. I still couldn't find the key. I was frustrated. My stomach began to cramp, and I had an urgent sensation to empty my bowels. I ran into the bathroom barely making it to the commode. When I finished, I continued to search the house for the key. I found it under the corn plant in the bathroom. I grabbed the key and contemplated my next move. I began to feel guilt, so I rearranged the pots in the kitchen, cleaned the refrigerator and mopped the kitchen again.

I grew tired of cleaning the house. I began to feel claustrophobic again. I had to get out of the house. My heart told me to stay home, but the obsession quickly took over. It's like I really didn't want to go. I knew I was harming myself and causing a great deal of pain to my family. I was cognitively aware of the pain I was inflicting on the people who loved me most, but my feelings were shut off. I couldn't actually respond to their pain. I could see Andreas cry and listen to him tell me how much he loved me. I know for assuredly he loves me, but I could not feel it. My feet started walking towards the door. I opened it and closed it again. The key without money was useless. I couldn't go to the bank anymore because he closed our joint accounts and opened new checking and savings accounts. I knew not to page Andreas and ask for money. He would want to know what I needed and then purchase it for me.

I called Aunt Mary. I acted as if I called to chat. She brought me up to date on some happenings I could have cared less about, but I pretended to be interested waiting for the opportunity to slip in a request for a $50.00 loan. I knew she would give it to me. I lied and told her I needed the money to buy diapers and milk for the baby.

Aunt Mary's house was very feminine with pretty, pastel colors. It was the complete opposite of her masculine appearance. She greeted me with a genuine, welcoming hug. As always, I enjoyed talking to her. My initial plan was to get the money and leave, but her presence was calming and peaceful; I almost forgot my motive for the visit.

"Where is the baby?"

"She is with her grandmother."

I didn't want to tell her everything. She knew I was not working and probably wondered why I didn't have my own baby. "Andreas prefers she stay with his mother during the day. He thinks I don't know how to care for her."

We talked about That Day. I can't believe I actually initiated the conversation.

"If I tell you something, would you please try very hard not to tell Grandma?" She didn't say anything, which meant I would have to take my chances. "I've been thinking about That Day." She looked at me. I continued. "You know when momma was killed." My eyes began to tear. "The day daddy did what he did. Aunt Mary I try so hard, but I can't get it off my mind. I can't stop thinking about it. I don't even know what happened to daddy. This may sound awful, but I want to find my daddy. I want to see him. I know what he did was wrong. I know what he did left me and my brother orphaned, but I also know he loved my mother."

"I know he did. I know he loved your mother too." I was surprised to hear Aunt Mary say this.

"I don't know what made him lose it like that. I just know Riley was Thelma's only child, and Thelma was devastated." I looked down feeling guilty because it occurred to me that I have never considered my grandmother's pain.

"You are so much like your mother. I know your grandmother may have not been what you wanted." She paused for a second pondering over what to say next. "Really no one could be your mother but Riley. Every time she sees you, you remind her of her loss. Can you imagine having to relive your daughter's death every time you see your daughter's child?" I really couldn't. Grandma and I never talked about momma or That Day. We acted as if it never happened. Actually, we never talked about anything. I never felt that Grandma took care of me out of love. I felt that she cared for me out of an obligation to my mother. I know she adored my mother, but I didn't feel that she loved me. Even before That Day, Grandma and I were always at odds. She really didn't like my daddy or anyone else who occupied momma's attention.

The urge to release my bowels returned. I wanted to take the money and leave. But I knew she would think that strange. Aunt Mary and I sipped tea and talked for a while longer. I

119

excused myself to the bathroom. When I came out of the bathroom, I thanked her for the loan and drove to the mall. I attempted to do something to distract myself from the crack house. I was trying very hard not to use, but the cravings were strong.

I took advantage of the ten-minute reprieve, when the cravings disappeared, and walked around inside of the mall. I used to love to shop, but fifty dollars wouldn't buy me the kind of stuff I liked. I went to a gallery and looked at work of other artists. I didn't feel like trying on clothes because I knew I would not be able to afford my taste in clothing with fifty dollars.

My stomach turned every time I thought about the fifty dollars in my pocket. I tried to walk it off. I tried to talk myself out of it, but my body was physically pained. My stomach felt as if it had turned inside out. I quickly exited the mall and headed for the car. My stomach cramped and a sharp, piercing pain permeated the left side of my head. I turned off the road and into the parking lot of a corner gas station and ran into the bathroom to empty bowels.

I was in route to Keekee's and Jazmyne's house still trying to talk myself out of it. I turned around three times and was almost home, but the compulsion took over. I turned into a fast food restaurant. I barely made it to the bathroom. I ran back to the car and drove to Jazmyne and Keekee's apartment. I wanted relief. I pulled into their driveway; I was so anxious that I shifted the transmission in park before the car had completely stopped.

Jazmyne and Keekee met me at the door. Keekee pushed Jazymyne behind him. He stood licking his lips and looking at me from head to toe with his now almost toothless smile.

"Girl, my brother let you out of the house and gave you the car too?"

"No, I found the extra key. Give me a dub." I gave Keekee twenty dollars. I smoked it in less than thirty minutes.

It still wasn't enough. So I bought another dub and then a dime. It wasn't enough.

"You need anything else?" Keekee stood behind Jazmyne rubbing his crotch. The scene was eerie, so I grabbed my bag and left. I was so high; I could hardly drive. I looked at my watch. It was 7:00; I prayed Andreas would not be home before I got there, but just like Rev. Deal used to say, "God always answers prayer, but sometimes the answer is no."
I started to drive off, but he opened the door before I could shift the transmission in reverse. I placed the transmission in park, turned off the engine, and got out of the car.

"Where have you been?" I closed the door to the car and walked through the patio door without answering him. His voice became louder, and he was oblivious to the neighbors who stopped in their tracks to see the sideshow. He grabbed my chin and looked in my eyes.

"You high, ain't you?"

"No."

"Then where were you?"

"I went to the mall, and I spent some time with Aunt Mary."

"I thought I took the car key."

"You did." I placed the key in his hand, as I walked passed him. "I found your extra key." I walked into the bedroom. I didn't have to look back to know that he was following me. I could almost feel him breathing on my neck.

"Where is Kyia?'

"She is asleep." He was still waiting for an explanation. I kept walking. I went in the bathroom and filled the tub with hot water. He sat on the bed, so I stayed in the bathroom to undress. He came into the bathroom while I soaked.

"Since when do you take baths? You always shower."

"Since today about three minutes ago." He picked up my panties, looked at the crotch area, and put it to his nose.

"When you finish doing whatever you are doing, please be so kind and close the door." I rolled my eyes and sunk down in the bathtub. He gave me a hard, long stare and walked out of the bathroom slamming the door behind him.

I soaked for a half an hour trying to bring myself down from the high. I began to feel remorseful. Andreas is a good guy and really didn't deserve this. My baby didn't deserve this shit either, but I honestly didn't start out with the intention of getting high. If he had left the baby, I wouldn't have done it. I would have stayed in the house and taken care of my baby. I got out of the tub, slowly dried my body, put on a t-shirt, and got into bed. He came into the room and turned on the light. I pulled the covers over my head. He slammed the nightstand drawers. Then he went to the dresser and to the closet slamming the doors as hard as he could. I knew he was trying to get on my nerves, but I didn't say anything.

I awakened at 3:00 in the morning and could not go back to sleep. I looked over my shoulder; Andreas was asleep. I went into the kitchen to get a glass of milk. We were out of milk. I went back to bed and tried to go back to sleep. I was not sleepy. That pungent, sweet, smell slowly entered my nostrils. Initially, the smell was faint but kept getting stronger and stronger. My stomach started to turn. I went into the bathroom and emptied my bowels. I went back to bed but still could not sleep.

I reached over and tried to awaken Andreas. He mumbled something, turned over, and went back to sleep. I went back in the bathroom to empty my bowels again. My stomach was cramping hard; I thought I would die. I slipped on my jeans and a sweatshirt, crept in the living room, and called Terri. I asked her to meet me at the corner. I was so sick that I should have called an ambulance. I quietly walked over to the dresser and got his wallet. He had thirty dollars. Initially, I was only going to take the money, but I saw his checkbook. I looked in the back of the checkbook and pulled out the last two checks. He is so meticulous; he would have remembered the last check number he used. I was fiending bad. The cravings were actually becoming painful. I grabbed my jacket and walked to the corner. I waited five minutes before Terri arrived.

"Girl, what's wrong with you?"

"Let's go to Jazmyne's and Keekee's house."

"You sure you want to go there? You know they cheap as hell." I knew what she said made sense. I heard Keekee and Jazmyne were both using, and nothing is worse than a dealer who is his best client. I knew I could get more for my money elsewhere, but they lived closer than anyone I knew.

"No girl I really don't want to, but I am craving so bad; I'm sick. Let's just go and get a hit from them and then we can go somewhere else."

It's almost 4:00 in the morning, and their lights were still on. People were walking out of the house looking like zombies. The drug is so evil and powerful that you quickly begin to look like the walking dead. Almost immediately after the first hit, an ashen layer coats the skin. It's the kind of ash you can't get rid of with lotion or even petroleum jelly. Karolyn, one of Jazmyne's friends, was still in the house. She answered the door. Her eyes were bulging, and she looked as if she had been up for a week.

"Is Keekee and Jazmyne here?" She stood in the door blocking the entrance.

"What you want to see Keekee for?" He came to the door and gave Karolyn a long, wet, and sloppy kiss. He stepped outside closing the door behind him.

"What's up?" He propped himself on the door while slowly rubbing his crotch.

"Give me a dub." I anxiously counted twenty, one, dollar bills.

"You know baby you don't have to pay for anything. Anything I got is yours. All you have to do is ask, and it will be given." I knew exactly what that meant. I found it hard to believe that someone so ugly could think this much of himself.

"Look I have money; you going to sell to me or what?"

"Who the hell you getting smart with crack head, stank, bitch?" His name-calling didn't bother me. All I wanted was a good hit.

"Are you going to sell to me? If not, I'll go elsewhere." He came close to me, grabbed me, and pushed me up against the door and began to fondle my breast. I screamed.

"I've been wanting you for a long time."

"Bitch, what you doing with my ole man." Jazmyne came outside and pulled him away from me. I was still in shock and speechless. I may be a crack head, but I still have taste. I wanted to tell her what happened and reiterate to her that she was probably the only woman on earth who wanted Keekee. Jazmyne was obviously stoned out of her mind, and I didn't think she would understand. She looked like pure hell. Her teeth were rotten and the fact that they were outlined in gold made them a focal point. She cursed me, but I really didn't understand what she was saying because all I wanted was a hit.

"I knew you been wanting to get with Keekee bitch. If you wasn't my niece's mother, I would kick your ass bitch." Although bitch is a one-syllable word, Jazmyne rolls it out of her mouth and manages to make it two syllables. I didn't say anything. I got back in the car with Terri, and we left. I wanted to curse Terri out because she didn't try to help me. I really was not surprised because you have no friends in this game. It is truly everyone for themselves, and the name of the game is, "*I am gonna get me me.*" I wanted to drop her, but I needed her to get around. We drove ten minutes to D380 and bought a gram for the $30.00. He gave us a $20.00 credit. It was not that he trusted us or even liked us; this is the way they reel you in. It's kind of like holding you hostage. You are free to roam, but when that craving hits; you come back to the dealer who cut you a little slack in hopes of getting something extra, but that rarely happens.

We went into one of his rooms in the back of the house. I was so anxious that I could not hold the pipe steady long enough to place the rock on the ashes. My legs were shaking and my stomach was turning so bad that I needed to clear my bowels again, but I had to get this first hit.

My muscles immediately relaxed. The sensation to release my bowel disappeared. My hands instantly stopped shaking. I was immediately calmed. The first hit feels good; it's a set up. The first one starts the chase, and you will never catch it again.

Everything was okay, and then the paranoia set in. I felt as if something was going down as if someone was plotting to harm me. What or who was out to hurt me, I didn't know, but it was a strong feeling.

"Come on Terri; let's go." She looked at me as if I were crazy.

"Where are we going?"

"Hell I don't know, but something is going down. We have to get out of here. They're watching us." I stared at the closet door. I quickly walked to the door and snatched it open. Of course, there was no one inside. I was paranoid; even though I didn't see anyone; my mind told me someone was there. I looked through the clothes that clumsily hang on shapeless wire hangers. I looked under old shoes that obviously have not been worn in this decade. My mind told me that someone was in the closet, and I believed it.

"Aw girl ain't nobody messing with us; we are the only people here. Sit down and relax." Terri had the pipe in her hand getting ready for another hit. I quickly grabbed my jacket and darted for the door. She reluctantly followed behind me; I had the money.

We got in the car and started driving. It was nine o'clock. The bank was open. I took out one of the checks and wrote it out to myself for $500.00. I signed Andreas' name and cashed it.

"You are dead. Don't go back home Thandisha; Andreas is going to kill you." Though she was laughing, I took her comment seriously. I knew he would be angry and would probably try to kill me if he found me. We drove past Keekee's house and decided against going inside; instead, we went to Norris' house.

Norris lived a block east of Keekee and Jazmyne. It seemed as if everyone in this neighborhood was drug affiliated. It was really a shame because the houses on this street were well maintained. Most of the lawns were perfectly manicured. The neighborhood was old, but the homes were sturdy. Original owners, elderly people who have lived here since the establishment of the neighborhood, occupied most of the homes. The drug dealer were usually their grandchildren, or in some cases their children, who for whatever reason got attracted to quick money and decided that a minimum wage job wasn't going to get it. Why work forty hours a week for $200.00 when you can make $500.00 in two hours?

Norris inherited his house from his grandparents. They raised him after his mother died. Norris is not as harsh as some of the other dealers in the neighborhood. I used to think he and Terri had a relationship, but then I found Terri really doesn't have relationships with anyone. With Terri, everything is about getting high, and she only socializes with people who can provide the means for her to get high.

Terri knocked on the door. It was about 9:30 a.m.; everyone in this game is usually asleep. It's a nocturnal game. You play all night and sleep all day. It took a couple of minutes for Norris to come to the door. Terri briefly spoke with him and walked back to the car.

"He's still working. What do you want to do? He says that we can stay here and hang out."

"Okay, that'll work. I gave her $150.00 to buy three grams." I got out of the car and walked into the house behind her. We walked into the living room, stepping over sleeping bodies that were probably crashed out for the day after smoking all night. We walked down a dark hall that reeked of urine into a back bedroom. I immediately locked the door and pulled out my pipe. I was calm still coming down from my first high. When I thought about it, it really was a waste of time. I get high for hours, but after the first hit, you don't get high anymore. You are simply blowing smoke and chasing after the first high that you will never get again. I constantly paced the floor. I knew I was getting on Terri's nerves.

"Girl, will you sit down?" I sat down. I was actually tired. My body was exhausted, but my mind was going a hundred miles per hour. I sat down and smoked some more; we must have smoked for five hours straight. When I looked in my pocket, I only had $60.00 left.

"Terri, give me my money. I know you got my fucking money!" She looked baffled.

"Thandisha, you are really tripping. You bought nine grams instead of three. Look in your pocket. She was right. I looked in my pocket, and I had five grams left.

"Girl, I'm tripping." We sat down and smoked and smoked and smoke. I was so tired that I fell asleep. Usually it's hard to fall asleep when you still have drugs. Even when you have smoked all of your dope, your heart is beating so fast that it is hard to calm down and actually sleep. I don't know how long I slept, but when I awakened, it was dark. I looked over my shoulder to find Terri deep in sleep. I was too tired to wake her, so I went back to sleep.

The sun, peeping through dark green, water stained curtains, awakened me. I didn't know the time, but I did remember going to sleep in the daytime and waking up in the middle of the night and now it was light outside again. I sat up and looked at the walls. I wasn't sure how long I had been here, but I knew that it was too long. I placed my hands in my pockets only to find them empty. I didn't have drugs or money. I placed my hands in my bra and found the other check.

"Terri, wake up." Terri was still deep in sleep. She didn't move.

"Terri! Terri!" I slid closer to her and pushed her shoulder back and forth in an attempt to awaken her. She grumbled but still did not wake up. I had money in my pockets earlier. I thought I had sixty dollars left. I was almost certain that I had more money. I was almost sure Terri took my money. She was the only person who knew I had money.

I nudged her again. She rolled over to her side.

"What?"

"Let's go."

"Where? Where do you want to go now?"

"I don't know; I just want to go." I sat for a second contemplating the next move

"Let's go to your apartment."

"I thought you were afraid Andreas would find you."

"I am sure Jazymne has already brought him to your place by now." We stood still half asleep. We stepped over the same bodies we stepped over when we came in.

"Thandisha, I am tired. I need another hit. You have anything."

"No, I'm all out."

"Let's go cash another one of those checks." I thought to myself, *How did she know I had another check?* She probably took my damn money, but the excitement of chasing a high again was overwhelming.

"Okay let's go." I kept looking at her out of the corner of my eye. Terri was very cunning and could not be trusted. We drove to the first Asset Capital Bank we saw. I was nervous. I thought to myself: *What if he knew I had taken money out of his account? What if he has already reported the checks stolen?* Initially, I was afraid of getting arrested, but the desire to get high was overwhelming, eradicating any fear of going to jail.

I stood in line and cashed the check. I know I must have had a bad body odor. I had not been home in at least two or maybe three days. I really couldn't remember if it was two days or three, and I had not bathed in as many days. I was self-conscious about my appearance. My hair was in long, thick, and unraveling plait that hang down my back; it was obvious I had not combed my hair. I looked at other women in the bank. They were neatly dressed with well-groomed hairstyles. In comparison, I looked a mess. My body odor was pungent, and my clothes were dingy and wrinkled. It was obvious that I was in need of sleep because darkened puffs surrounded my eyes.

I placed my identification on the counter and presented the check to the teller. I was nervous as hell on the inside, but I was able to hold a trivial conversation. She entered the check numbers into her computer. I was relieved when I saw her place the check in the stamp machine. She counted five, crisp one hundred dollar bills and placed them in my hand. I placed the money in my bra and exited the bank. I wanted to run to the car. My mind was telling me it was a trick. I was relieved when I left the bank's parking lot without being followed by policemen or bank security guards.

We went to Keekee and Jazmyne's house and bought a slab then drove to the liquor store and purchased a bottle of cognac. By the time we got to Terri's house, we were both craving like crazy. We were shaking so badly that we could hardly walk. My stomach cramped; the pain permeated the entire lower half of my body. I had emptied my bowels so much that I doubt if there was anything left in my intestines. The first hit immediately calmed both of us down. It took a lot of hits before we could talk again. We were hitting back to back on a hopeless chase for our first high. We were so engulfed in getting high that it took a while for us to respond to the knock on the door. Terri and I were looking at one another hoping that the other would stop smoking and answer the door.

Terri finally placed her pipe down and answered the door. It was Jazmyne with Keekee standing close behind her licking his lips and eyeballing me as if I were a tasty lollipop.

"Well ain't you going to invite us in?" Jazmyne stood in the door with her hands resting on what used to be big, voluptuous hips.

"No I'm not."

"What you mean you ain't going to invite us in? Hell I could put an end to this damn party. I hear Thandisha is spending money like water. I'll call my brother. I'm sure she stole the money from him because I know neither one of ya'll whores could have sold enough ass to be buying like everybody say ya'll is."

"Jazmyne, you can stay if you want, but Keekee ain't bringing his stank ass in my house, and I don't care who you call."

"Terri, why come he can't stay?" Jazmyne looked stupid. What I thought were gold teeth were not gold after all but tarnished, gold colored metal.

"Fuck you bitch, we ain't gotta stay here in this rat trap. Come on Thandisha; girl, let's go."

"I'm going to stay here." I agreed with Terri. Keekee was bad news. I was in a catch 22. I did not want Jazmyne and Keekee's company, nor did I want Jazmyne to tell Andreas where I was. She was right I had stolen the money from Andreas, and I wasn't ready for him to find me and end my party. I walked Jazmyne to the door and placed a dub of crack in her hand. With Jazmyne and Keekee gone, Terri and I were free to continue our party.

I began to feel guilty. I had not been home in two or three maybe four days. I was smoking to keep from coming down. I didn't want to feel the guilt. When I smoked crack, I knew I wouldn't feel anything, but no matter how much I smoked, I was no longer getting high. I was simply blowing smoke.

I gathered my things and went to the first bus stop I saw. Terri came out of the house calling my name begging me not to leave. It wasn't that she enjoyed my company; I had money. I didn't look back; I continued my route to the bus stop. When the bus came, I didn't bother to ask the driver his destination. As long as it went to a train station, I knew I could get home. That's one of the advantages of living in Atlanta; all of the buses eventually stop at a train station. The high quickly wore off. I was beginning to feel remorse. I could not remember how long I had been gone.

I could smell myself. Although it was not hot outside, I was drenched with perspiration. I smelled a strong stench on my skin. I was in desperate need of a shower. I didn't know exactly what I was going to tell Andreas. I knew that I couldn't say I was at the mall; besides, he already knows. I have broken so many promises to him. I know he loves me, but I honestly can't help myself. If I could do better, I believe that I would. At this point, I am totally powerless to this drug.

Crack cocaine knows my name, my social security number, and my DNA pattern. It has all of the control. Even when I say that I am not going to use, when it calls my name, I am totally helpless. I don't want to be at its mercy, but I am helpless. I can't seem to fight it. It starts with a smell that slowly creeps in my nostrils. Initially, it is a subtle aroma then increases to a strong pungent but sweet smelling odor. I could be simply washing the dishes, and it comes after me; no matter how hard I fight, it always wins.

The train was crowded. It must have been the morning rush hour. I was self-conscious about my appearance. I could smell myself, so I knew the passenger next to me could smell me too. I tried to keep my arms down and keep still in an attempt to keep my odor subdued. I was scared but relieved when I arrived at my stop.

The apartment was around the corner from the bus stop. I walked as slowly as I could trying to think of what I would say when I saw him. I decided that I would simply tell the truth, and we could take it from there.

The apartment was very quiet. The only noise came from the television in our bedroom. I walked down the hall. The door was slightly open. I slowly entered the bedroom. Andreas was asleep. I walked closer to the bed. A slim curvaceous body was snuggled next to him. I pulled the covers back. Dee groggily looked at me. I placed the covers back and left the apartment.

I was too upset to cry. Of all of the women in the Atlanta Georgia, he had to fuck my ex-best friend's sister. I walked out of the room and closed the door. I walked back to the bus stop. Just as the bus arrived, I saw Andreas standing on the patio in his robe. I boarded the bus. I didn't start out with the intention of going back to Terri's, but somehow that is where my feet took me. She opened the door, as I was getting ready to knock.

"Hey girl, you back?"

"Yeah, I'm back."

"Well come on in. I have a run to make, but I will be right back."

The apartment was quiet. It actually had the potential to be a nice apartment. It looked old and run down on the outside, with abandoned cars, old furniture and remnants of household trash covering the landscape. It was obvious that the landlord's only interest was the arrival of the monthly rent check. On the inside, the apartment had potential. It was clean and decorated with thrift store furniture, but it was neat. If it weren't for the half dressed dolls and a couple of children's books, I could easily forget that Terri had children. The oldest two now lived with her grandmother. Although the youngest two have different fathers, Derrick, Terri's last boyfriend, took them both. She was in the process of losing the children to child protective services, so she gave them to relatives. It was rumored that she persuaded her oldest, the nine year old, to perform oral sex on D380 for a twenty dollar rock. I was surprised that she showed no remorse. Nothing changed. Terri's routine remained the same. Her daily agenda was finding the ways and means to get high.

I was almost asleep when she came back. She was gone for a couple of hours. She came back with Keekee, Ron, Cedric and Jazmyne. I was uneasy when I saw them. Terri always acts as if she hates Keekee. I could understand her bringing Ron and Cedric. Ron is a drug dealer and Cedric is his sidekick, but I didn't understand why Keekee was there.

"Hey man, let's fire up some Yay." I knew that Keekee was smoking now, but I thought he and Jazmyne were still trying to keep that on the down low. It was almost shocking to see him jumping for a hit like a regular dope fiend.

"Wait a minute man. Hell chill out. You already owe Ron $200; you need to make good on that."

"I told you man; I'll have your money tomorrow."

"Yeah you need to have my money, and I want cash. Jazmyne's pussy done got old." Ron and Cedric were laughing giving each other high fives. Keekee was laughing but his laugh did not look genuine. He was smiling, but his facial affect was flat and expressionless.

"Ron, you so crazy." Jazmyne laughed. I found it hard to believe that she would find this funny.

"Thandisha, don't you have some money?" Terri knew I had money earlier.

"I got a couple of dollars." Actually, I had $100 in my pocket, but I wasn't going to tell Terri how much money I had. The scene made me nervous.

"I got $25 on a gram." This was a surprise since Terri never has money. I went in with Terri to buy a gram. Of course, we had to share with Keekee and Jazmyne. I almost couldn't get high looking at Keekee. He acted as if he had been smoking crack all of his life. A gram is a nice amount of dope for one person, but it wasn't enough for four crack smokers. We finished the gram in no time. I focused on Keekee. He acted strange. He was in the corner with Ron almost begging for another hit. Jazmyne was on Cedric treating him as if he were God. It didn't seem to bother her that Keekee was in the room. When I saw Ron with his pants down standing in front of Keekee who was on his knees, I almost threw up. I had to leave. I had to go. I grabbed my bag and headed for the door.

"Hey little momma, where you going?" Cedric pushed Jazmye out of his way and walked towards me.

"Excuse me!" I tried to look tough. "You talking to me?"

"Yeah I am talking to you. You smoked some of my dope too. You need to pay one way or another." I knew what this meant.

"Look motherfucker, I paid for my dope! I don't owe you shit!" I attempted to get my bag and leave again. He slapped me so hard that I could hear bells ringing in my ear.

"Bitch, you ain't leaving till I say you are." I started to panic. I wanted to scream, but in this neighborhood I doubt if anyone would care. I screamed for Terri to help, but she was in the kitchen getting high and totally oblivious to me. Cedric slapped me again knocking me on the floor. He grabbed a hand full of my hair and pulled me back on my feet.

"Look Ron; she is kind of pretty." Ron walked towards me pulling up his pants looking straight in my face.

"Oh this that bitch Jazmyne's uppity ass brother been looking for."

"Hell it sure is. Damn she looks good."

"Come on man let's take her ass for a ride." They gave each other a high five laughing while pulling me out of Terri's apartment. I kicked and screamed fighting with everything I had. I felt helpless. I have never been this frightened before. I was crying, pleading, and begging. We were almost to the car when I heard a loud bang

"What the fuck?" They immediately let me go.

"Leave her alone!" I couldn't believe this was Keekee actually helping me.

"Boy is you crazy? Get your whimp ass over here and suck my di..." I heard two consecutive, rapid gunshots and then Cedric fell to the ground with blood pouring out of both knees.

"Look who on their knees now." Keekee laughed like a mad man. His eyes were sad, but he laughed so hard I thought that I could actually see his tonsils.

"Wait a minute now Keekee, man, don't take this shit so seriously." Ron walked towards Keekee pleading with his hands up. Keekee pointed the gun straight at Ron.

"Go on Thandisha! Get out of here!" He motioned for me to go. I turned around and ran. I heard a third gun shot. I stopped, but I didn't look back. I kept running. I didn't exactly know where I was going. I just ran until I saw a bus stop. I had to sit still and try to figure out what happened. I prayed that Keekee hadn't killed anyone, but grateful he didn't allow Ron and Cedric to hurt me.

I was too afraid to stay at the bus stop. I ran to the phone booth. I didn't know who I was calling; I just dialed numbers. I was relieved when I heard Grandma's voice.

"Thandisha, is this you?"

"Yes Grandma, I need help. I am in trouble. Can you please come and get me?"

"Where are you?"

"Grandma, I don't know. I don't know where I am."

"What do you mean you don't know? What is wrong with you? Are you high on that stuff again? Andreas told me that you are using that crack stuff. He said that you stole his money." I didn't respond.

"Grandma, someone tried to hurt me. Please can you come and get me?"

"Well where are you?"

I looked up and saw the name of the street. "I am on Caitlyn Avenue Grandma. I am on Caitlyn."

"Well Caitlyn Avenue is a long street, and it's too late for me to come there. Call me in the morning, and I will meet you somewhere." Grandma hung up the phone. I didn't know where I was or where I was going to sleep. I had grown comfortable sleeping in dope houses, but I was terrified; I didn't want to go back to Terri's house. I had never slept in the street. I was cold. I was scared. I walked behind a dumpster and sat still. I was hiding, but I didn't know who I was hiding from. Everyone was a threat. I was too afraid to sleep. I squatted behind the dumpster waiting for the sun to rise. Eventually, I dozed off; when I opened my eyes, it was light outside.

I was relieved when the first bus arrived. I ran across the street, oblivious to the traffic, towards the bus stop. The driver looked at me and kept driving. I am sure that I looked a mess. I walked to the gas station at the corner of the street and went into the bathroom. I was right; I was a mess. My hair was all over the place. My eyes were bulging and surrounded by dark colored bags. My face had a grayish complexion accented by sunken cheeks. I pulled my hair back with my hands, walked back to the bus stop, and waited for the next bus.

I rode the bus to the train station then transferred to another bus and went to Grandma's. I waited down the street until Khalid left for school before I knocked on the door. I didn't want him to see me like this.

"Hi Grandma," she didn't respond. She simply looked at me with a blank stare. She didn't invite me in. I had to lightly push the door open and walk around her to get inside of the house.

"Grandma, I know I'm a mess." She didn't say anything she stood with her arms folded unable to take her eyes off of me.

"Grandma, I've been sick. Andreas was right. I am addicted to cocaine." I wanted to say crack, but if I admitted that I was using crack, then I had no hope of her helping me. People react worse to crack though it is a derivative of cocaine. I wanted to cry to help persuade her to take me serious in my quest for her help, but I still couldn't feel all of my emotions. She stood still in the doorway staring at me.

"I would like to get some help. Maybe I can go to a treatment facility or something. I've heard that people go to those places when they are sick."

"With what?" She laughed. "Thandisha, I don't have insurance on you anymore. Remember you refused to go to college, so your insurance benefits stopped when you turned 19."

"Grandma, I need help. Someone tried to kill me. I have been on the streets for three maybe four or five days. I don't even know exactly how long."

"Well what happened between you and Andrea?"

"You mean Andreas."

"Whatever, he said that you had been gone for over two weeks."

"We had a difference of opinion." I didn't even want to address how long I had been gone because the truth was I did not remember.

"He said that you were on drugs, and you left the baby."

"That's almost true."

"Well what part is true?"

"I guess all of it Grandma. Only I didn't intend to leave my baby." She continued to look at me with the blank stare.

"Grandma, I want to be honest. I am an addict. I am sick. I need help. Can I please stay here until I figure something out?"

"I don't know Thandie; you have to be able to follow my rules. You and I both know that is not possible. You do things the way you want to do them."

"Grandma, will you please just give me a chance? I mean just long enough for me to get a job and a place to live. She never said that I could stay, but she didn't tell me to leave. I wanted to stay long enough to rest if I couldn't get professional treatment.

I went to my old room. I was so tired that I could barely walk. I went through the closet. Grandma never changes. She never throws anything away. I found an old shirt. I went to the bathroom and showered. The water was purifying. I felt cleansed. I sat in the tub for several minutes before drying myself. I went back into my old room and fell asleep.

270^0
Two Hundred and Seventy Degrees

I felt a soft, warmness brush across my cheek. It was not flesh but a soft, comforting warmness. The touch, light as a feather, stimulated the surface of my skin.

"Thandie," the voice was familiar. It was soft and raspy as if it were plagued with laryngitis. I was not afraid. I didn't feel threatened. I knew this voice.

"Momma, is that you?" I sat up in my bed to look for more detail, but all I could see was a cloud-like form.

"Hi baby; it's me. I am only here for a little while. I came to tell you that it is okay now. You don't have to hurt yourself anymore." I was beginning to think I was dead or dying. I touched my face, and it still felt the same. I placed my hand on my heart; I could still feel its rhythm. I reached out to her, but I could not feel her; there was only the cloudy form.

"Why are you hurting yourself? Do you think this is what I want for you?" She used the same matter of fact tone she used when reprimanding me when I was younger. "I was taken away to make you stronger. It was my time. I want you to forgive yourself for whatever you feel you have done that would cause you to bring this pain in your life. I have forgiven you. God will forgive you. All you have to do is ask. Ask him Thandie, and he will forgive you."

I immediately began to cry. I knew this was my momma. I could not see her, but I could feel the comfort, the

139

same comfort I felt before That Day. I longed to feel her arms wrapped around me. I wanted to touch her soft, pecan, brown flesh. I wanted more than this cloudy form.

"Momma, it's you. Momma, oh God, you're back. I prayed for a long time for God to bring you back. You're here." I moved closer to the form.

"Momma, I have been so bad. I have done so many bad things." I sobbed so profusely that I could barely talk. "I am addicted to crack cocaine. I have neglected my family. I have brought shame to my brother."

"I know. I saw. I feel your pain, and that's why I am here to tell you that it's okay now. You can go on. You don't have to hurt yourself anymore. I am happy here. My spirit is at peace. Everything that happened was supposed to happen. It was declared before I was born." I listened closely to her words. The words were not what comforted me the most. It was the voice. Her raspy voice was always calm and gentle.

"Your brother loves you; you can never bring shame to Khalid. Even your addiction to crack cocaine, does not make your brother ashamed of you." The form began to disintegrate.

"Thandie, I have seen you grow into a beautiful woman and fall in love with a great guy. I have seen my beautiful grandbaby. I know you love her, but you have to stop hurting yourself. It was not your fault." The hand that was not actually a hand but a cloudy outline of a hand moved closer. It was warm and soothing. The form came closer and lay on the bed next to me the way momma used to. She had a way of lying on her side with her body slightly curved like a model or movie star.

"Remember I am still here with you, and it's okay." The form was gone, but the feeling of peace was still present. I was still calm and comforted.

"Momma," I called out to her, but the soft, raspy voice did not answer. The form disappeared, but I did not feel alone. I looked at the clock; it was 7:30 a.m. I was not tired. I was relaxed. I knew I was not dreaming. My momma was here, and she told me that everything was okay. I felt refreshed. I had not felt this good in a long time. At least at this moment, I did not have the desire to use drugs. I felt good and strong enough to look at my life and go back three hundred and sixty degrees to That Day when my daddy shot and killed my momma. I could face it now. Momma said that I had to forgive myself and ask God to forgive me. I dropped to my knees, and I prayed. I asked God for forgiveness for having anger towards him. I asked for forgiveness for having no faith, and I prayed for the strength to face my fears, my pain, and myself.

I sat still and enjoyed my new peace. I then showered, washed my hair, and twisted it in a tight bun. I found a pair of old jeans in the closet and borrowed one of Khalid's sweaters. The jeans were baggy. I was always petite but lost a lot of weight while using crack. After I got dressed, I sat on the edge of the bed engulfed in this new aura of peace. I knew God heard my prayer. There was no battle within me. I felt a sense of peace for the first time since my daddy killed my momma.

I went to the kitchen and made toast, sat at the table, and read one of Grandma's magazines. It amazed me how everyone in the pages appeared happy. I wanted happiness too. I wanted to smile again; not a superficial smile but a smile that came from my soul.

I needed a job, so I could take care of myself. Someone has always taken care of me. Although my inheritance would be coming soon, I needed to support myself until my 20th birthday. I wanted my own place to live and feel comfortable living alone. The house was big enough for me to live in, but I knew the healing process would be better if I lived on my own. Though God has forgiven me, I knew that it would take Grandma longer to forgive me.

Khalid was awake lying in his bed watching television when I walked passed his room. Grandma finally allowed

Khalid a voice in decorating his room. The walls were still adorned with my art, but he finally had age-appropriate furniture. I didn't like that he slept on a futon mattress, but I liked the flashing lights he placed in the ceiling as well as the acrylic framed posters of pretty girls and hip-hop stars.

"Hey Sis, what's up?" I stood in the doorway of his room. He was no longer a child but a young man. I felt the need to give him his privacy. "Have you eaten breakfast?"

"Yeah I made toast."

"Man I am kind of hungry myself." Not only did I enjoy talking to him, I enjoyed looking at him and admiring his maturity. He has a very gentle spirit unlike the young guys I had grown accustom to interacting with when copping my drugs. I followed close behind him, as he went into the kitchen. He opened the refrigerator, reached for the gallon of milk, and placed it on the table. A sudden sadness came over me. I missed so much time with him, but he acts as if nothing has happened. He still shows me respect and love. When he first saw me after coming back to Grandma's house, he was speechless. I was a mess. I had lost a lot of weight, and a gray, ashen coating covered my skin. He didn't say anything, but I could look at his expression and tell he was shocked, but after I rested, he came into my room and talked to me without judgment.

"Are you going to drink the whole gallon?"

"No just half of it." He laughed. I know momma would be proud. Khalid is not only handsome, but he is smart. He still makes all A's, and he is involved in extra curricular activities at his school.

"Khalid, I am so sorry. I am sorry for not taking care of you. I know you have heard bad things about me; some of them are probably true. I am sorry." My eyes were slowly filling with tears.

"Thandisha, you don't have anything to be sorry about. I feel bad I wasn't old enough to protect you and take care of you;

I don't care what anyone says or said about you. You are a star to me, and I am not talking about a rock star either." We both laughed. Rock star is one of the many street synonyms for crack addict because the drug looks like little rocks.

"But seriously Thandie, it has been a long time. I made peace with momma's death a long time ago. Don't get me wrong. I still have the bad dreams. I still have bad days. I still miss her. For a long time, I didn't allow myself to like girls because of what happened."

"Yeah right as handsome as you are Khalid, I have a hard time believing that." He looked serious.

"No seriously Thandisha for a long time I was afraid that I was like daddy. I was afraid that I could kill. I didn't allow anyone to get close to me like maybe there was a gene that could cause someone to kill, but then I realized that I wanted a fine honey to take to the movies and out to eat. I realized that daddy's behavior was his not mine. Momma came to me in a dream; I guess it was a dream. It seemed so real. She told me she was okay. She told me that I was okay that I didn't have to worry." I couldn't believe it. I didn't tell Khalid about my experience. But it was comforting to know I wasn't crazy, and she was actually here with me.

"Thandie, I don't know if you can handle this, but daddy writes me."

"What?" I was shocked. I didn't think he would have the desire to communicate with daddy. He was a momma's boy, and I was a daddy's girl.

"Grandma doesn't know, and I understand it may upset her, so I don't tell her."

"Where is daddy?" I was not interested in Grandma at the time. I wanted to hear more about daddy.

"He is still in prison, but he gets out in three years."

"Do you write each other often?"

"Yeah, at least every week."

I was proud of my little brother. He was smart and mature. He had a transcending calmness. I wanted to ask for the address, but I didn't have to. He went into his room, came out with a box of letters, and gave them to me.

"Thandie, if you want to read them, you can; I understand if you don't want to read them. I want to tell you one more thing."

"What's that?"

"I want you to know that I love you more than anything on earth. I remember how brave you were the night momma was killed; I understand if life has been too much for you, but I want you to make peace with God and make peace with yourself." His eyes were filling with tears. I punched him in the arm. He stood and hugged me before returning to his room.

I enjoyed the family reunion with Khalid, but I had to start looking for a job. I went back into my old room, put on my shoes, and left for the store. I passed Ayanna's house. I wanted to stop and see her parents, but I was ashamed. Ayanna is in college, and she is probably doing very well. I would have loved to see Mrs. Williams, but I still looked a mess. I didn't want her to see me like this. I walked to the store and purchased a newspaper. I took my time walking back. I was truly enjoying myself. It was as if this was the first time I had ever walked these streets. I could smell the taste of freedom. Although I was still sick, the chains of my addiction felt lighter.

When I returned from the store, Grandma looked at me strangely. She was getting out of the car with bags in both hands. I knew what she was thinking. I am not trying to make myself at home here. I knew she would not allow that to happen. I had slept for two days when I first got here, and when I awakened, all of the bedroom doors had dead bolt locks on them. I couldn't get offended. Just because I had not stolen from her didn't mean that I wouldn't. When you are on drugs, anything is possible.

"Where have you been?" Although she asked this question accusingly, I was so happy that I did not get offended. No one was going to steal my joy today.

"I just came back from the store to get a newspaper. I am going to look for a job today. Let me get your bags." She was reluctant. I guess she was afraid that I was going to steal the bags. I carried the bags into the house, sat down, and read the newspaper. I circled jobs of interest. She watched me as if she were waiting for me to do something crazy. I ignored her and continued to read. Khalid left the table shaking his head in disbelief. We made eye contact and gave one another a reassuring smile.

I made phone calls. Finally, after several "No we are not hiring" responses, I was given an appointment for an immediate interview at CNR Bookstore. I didn't have anything modern and up to date to wear, but I found an old suit in the closet. I showered and applied some of Grandma's makeup to my face. Although my color was coming back, I still had a light ashy coating on my skin.

"Grandma!" I knocked hard; it took a while for her to come to the door.

"Where do you think you are going?" Her accusing tone caught me off guard, but I didn't allow it to get next to me.

"Grandma, I have a job interview today. I am going to CNR Bookstore. I'll be back later."

"Wait a minute." She closed the door leaving me outside for several minutes then came out of her bedroom fully dressed with her purse in her hand.

"Khalid, I'll be back. I am taking Thandisha to her job interview." I didn't say anything. I really didn't feel like walking to the bus stop and waiting on the bus anyway. We drove in silence. There was a lot I wanted to say to her, but with Grandma there is always a shield. She never lets you totally in.

Grandma parked the car while I went into the bookstore for my interview. The bookstore was humongous. There was a coffee shop on one side and several shelves filled with books on the other. I knew this was my job. I could feel it. I checked in with one of the sales clerks at the counter.

"Hello, my name is Thandisha Glaze. I have an interview with Cersi Hunter." A young, modern, dressed woman came from behind the counter.

"Hello, I am Cersi." She extended her hand and embraced mine with a firm, confident handshake. I gave a firm handshake in return and followed her to an office in the back of the store. She interviewed me for thirty minutes. She and I had the some of the same interests. I was surprised when she offered me the Purchasing Coordinator position instead of the Sales Clerk position. Ten dollars an hour was not a lot of money, but it was enough to get established. I shook her hand again and thanked her. It was Thursday; we agreed I would start on Monday. When I walked out of her office, Grandma was entering the bookstore. She gave me an *I know you did some fucked up shit, and I ain't forgot it* look. I walked out smiling. I gave Grandma a hug; she was initially resistant, but she reluctantly embraced me.

"Grandma, I got the job!"

"Well that's good, but don't get too excited; a sales clerk is not going to take care of you and a baby you know."

"I didn't get the Sales Clerk position. She hired me as a Purchasing Coordinator."

"Well do you have to deal with money?" I knew where she was going.

"Actually, I don't. I will be ordering books and arranging book signings." She appeared slightly impressed. I really didn't care one way or the other. I knew it was all going to be okay.

I needed clothes. I had clothes at Andreas'. I had not talked to him in a couple of weeks. Our last encounter was so painful; I did not bother to contact him again. I have not seen my daughter in a while. He decided I was not good enough for Kyia. I guess I decided the same. I was tired of Kyia seeing me high. She may not have known I was high, but I knew. The guilt I felt was overwhelming. I can't believe some of the stuff I did like leaving her at home alone. I told Andreas that I was gone for only a couple of hours. Actually, I was gone all day. I initially had planned on getting a hit then coming home, but after that first one, I could not leave. It was as if my feet were glued to the floor. I didn't leave until I had spent all of my money. It's amazing; I am just now feeling guilty about it. The image of Kyia alone in the house constantly flashed in my mind. I pray she will forgive me

"Hello."

"Andreas?"

"Yeah, what do you want?" He was nasty, but I expected it. I am sure that I deserved it. Khalid is the only person who loved me enough to feel my pain and hold me accountable for my actions without constantly trying to make me feel bad.

"How are you?"

"Thandisha, I have to go. I am busy. If you are calling to see Kyia, don't bother to ask. The answer is no." Everyone was trying my patience, but thank God for this new shield because it was not working.

"Actually Andreas, I need to get my clothes. I start a job Monday." He was silent. I knew he didn't believe I was working. I am sure as I felt doomed to a life of using drugs, he probably believed my life was doomed also.

"I don't have any of your clothes."

"What do you mean? I have clothes in the closet, the dresser, and the armoire. You didn't throw my armoire out did you?" I prayed he didn't throw it out because that would have driven me over the edge. It belonged to my mother, and it was very dear to me.

"No, the armoire is still here. I gave it to Kyia. I could hear a soft, feminine voice in the background. It sounded like Dee, Ayanna's sister, but I wasn't sure.

"Then where are my clothes?"

"I don't know and really don't give a damn!" He hung up the phone. I began to panic. I could not believe he threw away my clothes. I had a nice wardrobe with many classy pieces. What was I going to do for clothes? I picked up the phone and dialed again.

"Andreas," he didn't say anything, but I knew he was on the phone. "Look I need my clothes. If you have them, please allow me to come over and get them, or bring them over to me if you don't want me in the apartment." Initially, he didn't say anything, but I knew he heard me.

"Didn't I just tell you? I don't have any of your shit!"

"I know what you said. I heard you loud and clear."

"Well is there anything else you want?"

"Actually there is, I would like to see Kyia."

"Well that ain't going to happen!"

"Andreas, I want to let you know that I am okay now. It may not be today, but I will see Kyia because I am her mother.

"Please don't fucking remind me Thandisha; I would rather forget!" He hung up the phone.

I panicked. Monday was only three days away. I didn't have clothes. I didn't have money. I could feel the depression settling in. The pungent odor was forcing its way into my nostrils. It was faint but growing in intensity. I went to my room and lay on the bed. The smell got stronger. My stomach began to cramp. I went to the bathroom to empty my bowels.

Khalid's door was slightly open when I came out of the bathroom. I lightly knocked on the door.

"Come in," he was lying on his futon and throwing a small basketball into a miniature basketball goal that was nailed to his closet door.

148

"Hey guy, what's up?"

"Are you okay Thandie?"

"It must be something I ate." I started crying. My baby brother pulled me close and held me tightly. I was always the one to comfort him, and now he was comforting me.

"Guess what?" I didn't allow him time to respond. "I have a job."

"Great, what kind of job?" He was excited for me.

"I am the new Purchasing Coordinator for CNR Bookstore. Well that's if I can find some clothes to wear."

"That's great Thandisha. That's really good. Then why are you crying?"

"Didn't you hear me? I don't have work clothes. Andreas threw my clothes away."

"We can go to the mall. I have money in the bank. I'll take you shopping; stop crying." The cravings were slowly leaving me. It's just as momma said, "It's okay now."

"What are you doing in here?" She looked at me as if I were ready to put the house in my pocket and walk out with it.

"I am talking to Khalid."

"Come here; I need to talk to you." I followed her into the den.

"I don't think it is a good idea for you to be all over the house and in everyone's room. You have your room, and that's where you need to stay." I didn't say anything, but I wanted to give her a piece of my mind. I was thinking to myself why allow me in the house to treat me so bad? She could have left me in the street and allowed strangers to do the job for her. I agreed to stay in my room and go no further than the kitchen and the bathroom.

After my talk with Grandma, Khalid came into my room; we were getting ready to leave for the mall to shop for my work wardrobe when Grandma saw us.

"Where do you think you are going?"

"Khalid and I are going to the mall. Andreas threw my clothes away. Khalid agreed to loan me money to buy a few pieces until I get my first check." Grandma went off.

"Khalid, go to your room!" We were both shocked.

"Why? What is wrong with you Grandma?"

"You are not going to buy her a damn thing! No one told her to get on drugs. She will get some clothes when she buys some." Khalid left the house slamming the door behind him. I was not going to give up. If I had to go door to door asking for clothes, then that is what I would have to do.

"And you," I looked around. There was nobody present but me. "You are walking a fine line, and don't forget it."

I went into my room and wrote out my plan. Getting the hell out of this house was my first priority. I wasn't actually mad at Grandma. After using drugs and socializing with addicts, I can understand why Grandma would feel uneasy around me. I understand her lack of trust towards me, but I am human and at this point, very fragile. Whatever the cost, I had to protect myself first.

If I saved my money, I could move within a month. I didn't need a big place. I just needed something big enough to accommodate Kyia and myself. I didn't know what Andreas was thinking, but I am sure he knew Kyia was going to be in my life. I hoped he knew I was going to see my child. I understand I hurt him, and I hurt the baby. No one could make me feel worse than I already do. I will do it right this time, and this time it will be solid.

I heard Khalid's car in the garage. He was gone for several hours. I knew Grandma made him angry. What she doesn't understand is regardless of what I have done, Khalid is my brother. We share the same pain. We have the same fears, and nothing and no one can come between us.

"Thandie?" He softly knocked on the door.

"Come in." He entered the room carrying several bags. "Here try these on, and see if you like them." I couldn't believe my brother had such good taste. The black suit was a good choice for the first day of work. I really didn't like the Khaki skirt, but I was grateful to have clothes for work. "Thank you so much Khalid." I gave him a big hug. My little brother had grown into a tall, muscular young man. I was proud of him. I was determined that I would also make him proud of me. It was awkward that we felt the need to whisper, so Grandma would not hear us, but that would eventually be okay. I accepted the fact she also needed time to heal.

I stayed in my room all day Saturday and Sunday. I was bored, but I didn't want more confrontation with Grandma. I did not have anywhere to go. I didn't have friends. The relationships you form in active addiction are superficial, based solely on one's ability to get drugs. I started writing myself little messages. I told myself everyday, "I am a beautiful person." Hopefully, eventually, I would believe it. My number one priority was to heal the relationship with my daughter. I have missed so much with Kyia.

I prayed that Andreas would forgive me. I know that I have caused him a lot of pain and disappointment. He acts as if he hates me. I take responsibility for my role in our break up, but it was not totally my fault. It was very hard for me to talk to Andreas. He is holding on to my recent past. What he does not understand is I was not capable, but I have a desire to right all of my wrongs, mainly the wrong that I did to myself.

315⁰
Three Hundred and Fifteen Degrees

I was awake, as usual, at sunrise. I was fresh and vibrant. I don't know if I actually slept, but I was awake and feeling good. I immediately jumped out of bed, fell to my knees, and gave thanks to the creator. I turned on the radio then went into the bathroom to shower. The water was purifying. I got out of the shower, slowly dried my body and lotioned with some of Grandma's perfumed lotion I found in the cabinet under the bathroom sink and dressed for work.

At 6:45, I was at the bus stop. I didn't have a purse, so I borrowed one of Khalid's book bags. The black suit Khalid bought me looked great. The shoes were sharp as hell. I arrived at the bookstore thirty minutes early; I walked to a nearby Deli, drank coffee, and read the paper to kill time. I was at the bookstore ten minutes before 9:00. Cersi greeted me, found a place for my things, and gave me a tour of the store.

Cersi and I shared the same office space, but we each had our own desk, which were five feet apart and separated by an Asian room divider. I was overwhelmed when I discovered that I had to learn to use the computer. I could type, but I didn't have software skills.

"Cersi, I don't know if you knew this when you hired me, but I have never used this software before. To be honest, I have

152

never even turned on a computer." I waited for her to thank me for coming and escort me out of the door.

"Don't worry about that; you will catch on. I didn't know how to use a computer either, but you quickly get the hang of it the more you use it. Besides, for the next two weeks, we will train." I was relieved. I really needed this job. I guess I really didn't need the money. I could basically flip burgers and live with Grandma until next year when my inheritance kicked in. But the job was a boost to my damaged self-esteem. It made me feel good on the inside. The job gave me a purpose. It was a catalyst for my transition back into mainstream society.

By lunchtime, I was tired; I could barely keep my eyes open. I didn't eat lunch; I wanted to make sure I had enough money to survive until payday. Instead of eating, I walked hoping to get some energy from the sun. Midtown was absolutely beautiful. I have been here before but never seen it with these eyes. I know the buildings were here probably before I was born, but I have never paid attention to them before. I continued to walk with no particular destination in mind. As I walked past the library, I saw Andreas' truck. I walked to the truck. I was hesitant, as I really didn't want negative vibes. He was concentrating on trimming hedges and did not see me.

"Hi." I tapped him on the shoulder.

"Hey, what are you doing down here?" He looked surprised to see me. He turned the hedger off and removed his eye protecting glasses.

"I told you; I am working now. How is Kyia?"

"She is doing well. She is in daycare now. She likes to play. Since there aren't kids at momma's house, I decided to put her in a childcare program."

"I am coming over Saturday to see her. I don't have to take her with me, but I am coming to see her."

"Who in the hell do you think you are?" His demeanor instantly changed. "You are not going to tell me when you are coming to see her! You have been hanging out off and on, and now you want to play mommy! I don't think so. If you will excuse me, I have to go back to work. I have a child to take care of." I grabbed his arm, as he turned away.

"Andreas, you know what I did; everyone and their momma probably know, but I am coming to see Kyia Saturday morning. I will be there by 9:00." I didn't give him a chance to say anything. I walked away.

It was 12:45, and my lunch break was almost over. I quickly walked back to work.

"Did you have a nice lunch?"

"Actually, I did; thanks for asking." I was eager to get back to work. There were books left on my desk that needed entering into the database. Cersi gave me a list of soon to be released books to order from the distributor. One of my responsibilities was to read the review copies of books by new authors and decide if they would sell well with our clientele. If a book was chosen as a good seller, it was my responsibility to order the book and promotional materials to market the books. It was also my responsibility to contact the authors for book signings. I had a lot of responsibility, and I loved it.

I was still working at 5:20. Cersi reminded me that we are off the clock at 5:00. I was so into my work that I forgot to look at the clock. I pulled out the instructions I had written down earlier so that I could shut down my computer. I grabbed my things and walked to the bus stop. I had a great day today. I looked strangers in the eye and felt no shame. When I smoked crack, I could not look anyone in the eye because I knew what I had become. I had become an empty shell willing to do almost anything for a hit. I did not care who was hurt in the process. I am so happy that at this moment I feel good enough. I feel worthy enough. I felt very much part of the mainstream.

Grandma was sitting in the den when I walked in the house. I greeted her, went into the kitchen, and made a sandwich. I felt uncomfortable in the kitchen. Grandma didn't say anything mean to me. Though I was in the kitchen, and she was in the den, I could still feel the negative vibes. I quickly ate my sandwich, went into my room, and undressed. I was tired; I showered and went to bed. When I awakened, it was 6:00 am again. I showered, dressed, and walked to the bus stop. I didn't feel as pretty as I felt yesterday. I wore the khaki pants and a white, cotton shirt. I thanked God that Khalid knew to buy basic black shoes. I looked forward to my first check, so I could add more basics to my wardrobe, take myself to a nice restaurant, and buy gifts for Kyia.

I arrived thirty minutes early again. Cersi's car was parked in its usual reserved parking space. I went around to the back and knocked on the door. She greeted me with a welcoming smile.

"Wow you're such an early bird. I'm going to give you a key, so you don't have to wait around outside if no one is here." I was initially afraid to take the key. It had been a long time since anyone trusted me like this. I had not trusted myself in a long time. I reluctantly took the key and placed it in my bag. I went to my desk, turned on my computer, and started my workday. The work was interesting. Cersi was a very good trainer. In just one day, I developed a thorough knowledge of book promoting.

"Cersi, have you ever thought of decorating the office with art?" I loved my workspace, but it was bland.

"Yes, actually there was art in here." She pointed to the holes in the walls.

"But when I bought my ex-husband out, he took the art with him. I have not had time to look for more."

"I have several pieces of art in my collection. I can bring them and if you like any of the pieces, I can donate them to the office."

"Well that won't be necessary. I can just give you what you paid for them."

"Actually, I didn't pay anything for them; I paint in my spare time. I've been told that I am a very good artist." She was excited about seeing my work. Now that I offered, I had no idea how I would get the pieces to work. I could ask Khalid, but Grandma would probably die if she saw me in his car.

I called Andreas on my break to see if he would consider giving me a ride to work and to see if he would bring some of the art I left at the apartment. I had a few nice pieces behind the armoire.

"Hello," I didn't expect to hear a female voice. "May I speak with Andreas?"

"Who's calling?" It sounded like Dee, Ayanna's sister.

"Can you tell him that it's Thandisha?" I heard arguing in the background. I could tell someone placed their hand over the phone because the sound was muffled.

"Yeah?"

"Hi Andreas, this is Thandisha."

"What do you want?" I hated when he attempted to make me feel like a microbe. Couldn't he see that I was making progress?

"I have some art in your apartment. I am sure that you didn't throw it away. I need it to decorate my office. I was wondering if you could bring it to the bookstore or maybe give me a ride to work in the morning because I have some pieces at home I would like to bring." He was silent. If it were not for the female cursing and screaming in the background, I would have thought he hung up the phone.

"What time?"

"I have to be at work at 9:00. Can you pick me up at 8:00?"

"Yeah," he hung up the phone without a good-bye. I didn't care. I had a ride to work.

I went back to work, finished entering the monthly sales data in the spreadsheet, and worked on a book promotion. Cersi was right; once you work with the computer, it becomes easy. The more you use it; the more comfortable you become with it. I didn't have money, so I window-shopped during lunch. The first thing I wanted to buy for myself was a purse. I was tired of carrying Khalid's book bag. I was beginning to feel cute, sexy and feminine again. I wanted a soft, feminine bag to carry my things. Cersi was my fashion inspiration. Even when she wore jeans, she made a fashion statement.

After lunch, the day went very fast. I was glad to see 5:00. I missed the first bus, so I waited thirty minutes for the next bus. I was an hour late getting home. Grandma met me at the door, as I entered the house.

"Where have you been?"

"I've been at work. I missed the first bus." She snatched the book bag out of my hand, opened it, and dropped all of its content on the floor.

"I am not going to have drugs in this house!" She bent down on the floor and went through all of my belongings. When she didn't find anything, she left everything on the floor and walked away mumbling. I was too angry to hear what she said. I sat on the floor, put my things back in the bag, and went to my room. I showered and prepared for work. I didn't eat dinner. I drank a glass of juice, ate fruit, and watched television.

I awakened at 2:00 in the morning hungry as hell. I went into the kitchen to get something to eat. Khalid was in the den talking on the phone.

"Hey sis what's up?" It was obvious; he was talking to a girl. He was sitting on the sofa, talking low, and smiling from ear to ear. He reminded me of Andreas. Andreas and I would sometime talk on the phone all night.

"What's up guy?" I made a sandwich and went back to my room. I was uncomfortable in this house. To be honest, I was never comfortable living with Grandma. It was never a home. It was simply shelter. I really looked forward to getting my own place. I looked forward to feeling totally free. Everything in my life was working out. I enjoyed my job at the bookstore. A stranger trusted me with the key to her business, but I was living like a convict at Grandma's house.

It was imperative that I get a place so that my baby could visit. I longed to see my baby. I missed Kyia. I may not have been a good mother, but God knows I love my baby. I am going to mend the relationship with my daughter. Her father was trying to prevent it, but I knew when Andreas realized that I was clean and making a change in my life, he would allow visits with Kyia.

I awakened depressed. I wasn't as eager to get out of bed. That 2:00 a.m. snack made me sluggish. I immediately fell to my knees and asked the creator to give me this day. That faint, pungent smell was in my nose. Initially, I thought of calling Cersi and requesting the day off, but the thought quickly left my mind. Last night, I dreamed I was using. The dream was vivid. It was so real that I awakened with a strong urge to clear my bowels. I didn't immediately get out of bed for fear my feet would take me somewhere that I really didn't want to go. Andreas would be picking me up, so I sat at the end of the bed and watched television before getting dressed. Grandma walked pass my room. Initially, she didn't say anything. I could tell she was looking at me, but I didn't look up. She went toward the kitchen and then came back to my room.

"It's 7:15. Are you going to work? You need to get ready. You are not going to lay your ass up in here all day." She was really pissing me off. I really wanted to curse her too, but she was my grandmother. Besides, I was determined I was going to stay and endure whatever she dished out until I had the finances to leave.

"I am going to work. Andreas is giving me a ride. I am taking some of my art to decorate my office." She quietly stood in my door for a second. I guess she could not think of anything insulting to say, so she left. I quickly showered and dressed for work. I gathered some of my art from the garage, sat in the living room where I had a good view of the driveway. Andreas arrived at exactly 8:00. He got out of the car and opened the trunk of his new SUV. I had to give it to him; he looked good. I met him at the door before he pressed the doorbell. I glanced at the window while getting in the car. Grandma stood in the window with a disapproving look on her face.

"Good morning."

"Good morning, did you bring Kyia?"

"I took her to school."

I hoped that I would get to see her, but I did tell him that I was coming over this weekend, and I still meant it.

"Thanks for the ride. I would have never made it with all of this on the bus."

"You look better than you did the last time I saw you." He was right. I knew I looked much better. The ashen coating that once covered my skin is now replaced by a soft glow.

"Thanks, I am trying. It gets hard at times, but this time I am going to make it. I am a little stressed right now, but when I get my first check, I can atleast buy clothes for work."

"I guess I shouldn't have thrown your clothes away."

"It would have been nice if you hadn't, but I am not going to cry over spilled milk."

"If you like, I can take you shopping this weekend." I wanted to tell him to go to hell, but I needed clothes.

"Are you sure your girlfriend won't mind? Wasn't that Dee who answered the phone?"

"I don't have a girlfriend. I have a friend. Besides, what difference does it make who it is?" He was right; besides I really didn't give a damn. I had too much work ahead of me trying to stay clean.

"Well I don't want to cause any problems for you. How is Kyia? I can't wait until Saturday. I don't have any money to buy her a present. All I have is bus fare until I get paid, but when I get my first check, I would like to take her shopping." I stared straight ahead, but I could tell he was looking at me. I knew he wanted to exert some control, but he had to give me my props. I was doing okay; at least, I was putting up a fight.

We arrived at the bookstore at 8:20. I didn't have to be at work for another forty minutes. I was happy when he offered to buy breakfast. I had not eaten out in so long. We ordered biscuits and juice, but for me it was like a sit down, wine, and dine meal.

"Damn Thandisha, you must have been hungry. I can remember when you would pretend like you wasn't hungry and your stomach would make hunger sounds like crazy." He was talking about our first date at the mall.

"Yeah well you see I'm not shy anymore."

"Yeah I see."

He drove back to the bookstore. I pulled out the key and opened the door while he brought the art into the office.

"You're moving up; they gave you a key. I am impressed." He sat the pieces down.

"What time do you get off work?"

"5:00."

"Well if you want to wait about fifteen minutes, I can give you a ride home. I am over this way today."

"Sure I would appreciate that." Since he gave me a ride to work too, I had an extra $3.00.

I spent the entire day on the phone making phone calls planning for next month's book signings. I confirmed times, dates, and made hotel arrangements. Reynolds Jordan was making her debut. She obviously had a big advertising budget. The Renaissance is a very prestigious hotel, but it wasn't upscale enough for her. I spent the day faxing over brochures from different hotels to her publicist. At the end of the day, she was not satisfied with any of the accommodations. The only thing confirmed was CNR's commission for the publicity.

The most rewarding event in my life today was lunch. I went to a sandwich shop and ate a baked potato with sour cream and chives. I ordered a glass of water, added lemons and sugar, and made lemonade. After lunch, I went back to the tedious task of trying to find hotel accommodations for Reynolds Jordan.

"You still have not found her a suitable place?"

"I'm trying, but she is very hard to please." Cersi looked disappointed as if I were not doing my job.

"Well what about the Renaissance?"

"I faxed the brochure on the Renaissance. She wanted something more upscale." Cersi appeared surprised.

"Well how much is her marketing budget a million dollars?" We both laughed. Her laughter restored my comfort zone. I needed this job, and I wanted to do a good job. I had not gotten to the level where my self-esteem was self-sufficient. I was still trying to please people. I wanted Cersi to like me and feel confident with my job performance. She came back to my desk.

"Oh I forgot to tell you; I love the art. You are a great artist. Why don't you try and sell some of your work?"

"I have thought about it. I need to find a place to sell it."

"Well, if you like, you can sell it by the coffee counter. Make some space for yourself, bring in one piece at a time, and see what happens."

"Wow, Cersi I'd love to do that!" I could not believe Cersi gave me an opportunity to sell my art. Andreas was always trying to get me to sell my art.

I faxed a copy of the brochure from the VIP Elite to Reynolds Jordan. Finally, she was pleased with the VIP Elite. I was surprised because the Renaissance was more convenient. It was close to the bookstore and was also walking distance to a few hot spots in town. Cersi appeared pleased the event was finally arranged.

I looked forward to going home today. I was tired. At 5:00 when I walked outside, Andreas was waiting.

"Hey girl," I returned his greeting with a slight wave, but I was more interested in the little head in the back of the car. I ran to the car and opened her door.

"Kyia!" She was so beautiful. Her hair was all over the place. I could tell Andreas tried to comb it, the parts in her hair were not uniform, and the barrettes did not match.

"Hi," She wasn't as excited as I would have liked. I unfastened her car seat and gave her a big hug. I didn't want to let her go. Her skin was soft. Her eyes were beautiful.

"How have you been baby?" She really wasn't looking at me.

"Kyia, daddy is going to take you to McDonalds." She didn't say anything, but she easily gave her daddy a big smile. I got in the car and sat in the back seat with her.

"Kyia, do you want momma to go to McDonalds with us?"

"Yes," I didn't know if she really wanted me to go, but I wanted to go. I was excited and nervous being with my child again. I could not think of anything or anyone you could love more than your child. Seeing Kyia reiterated to me that I was once loved and that I am still loved. Only a God who loves me could allow me to produce a child as beautiful as Kyia.

We stayed at McDonalds for two hours playing and talking. The longer I was with Kyia, the more she interacted with me. I knew she couldn't verbalize her feelings, but I knew it was painful to have a mother one day and be motherless the next day. I vowed to make it up to her.

"Thandisha, this has been fun, but I need to get Kyia home, so she can go to bed." I knew he was right, but I wanted to spend more time with her. I truly enjoyed the evening with my daughter. I was almost in tears when he fastened her in the car seat. I sat in the front seat with Andreas. I didn't want Kyia to see me cry. Andreas touched my shoulder reassuring me that everything would be okay. I would have felt better; however, if he would allow me more time with my daughter.

I continued to sit in the car for several minutes after we arrived at Grandma's. I didn't want to say good-bye to Kyia. He didn't turn the engine off, so I knew he was ready to leave. I walked around to the back of the car, opened the door, and kissed her. She gave me what felt like a genuine hug and waved good-bye.

"Thanks Andreas, I had a great time." I turned away and walked towards the house.

Aunt Mary's car was in the driveway. Before I could enter the house, Grandma met me at the door and blocked my entrance. Aunt Mary stood close behind her.

"I told you once; I was not putting up with anymore of your shit. Where have you been?" I looked at the clock. It was 7:30. I usually get home by 6:00.

"I was spending time with my daughter."

"I know what kind of car Andreas drives. You got out of a truck."

"Andreas has a new truck. It's the same truck he was in this morning when he came for me."

"I doubt very seriously if he would allow you around Kyia." I was trying to stay at Grandma's for three more weeks, but I could tell it was not going to work. Grandma thought she was tired of me, but I was equally tired of her.

"Grandma, everyone is not like you. Some people are forgiving." She stood in the door as if she were not going to allow me in the house. I looked at Aunt Mary. Her facial expression confirmed this was the plan.

"I think that it is best that you go on and move."

"How can I move Grandma? You know I won't have money until I get paid on Friday."

"Not having a money or a job never stopped you in the past from finding a place to lay your head." I was hurt and angry at the same time. I didn't know which emotion to react on; both were equally as strong.

"Can I come in and get my things?" She had my things packed in a black garbage bag and passed them to me through the door.

"Can I say good-bye to my brother?" I made an attempt to walk in the house. She stepped in front of me again blocking my entrance.

"He is not here." It was useless, so I took my belongings and left. I didn't know where I was going. It was dark. I was scared. I didn't want my feet to take me anywhere that was detrimental to my shaky foundation. The bus ends its last route in this neighborhood at 7:00. Wherever I was going, my feet would have to get me there.

I turned around and contemplated knocking on the door again to ask one more time if I could stay for the night, but the thought of looking into Grandma's face made me ill. I crept around the back of the house to the laundry room and used my driver's license to open the door. I put my things down and climbed on top of the washer and dryer and went to sleep. It was an uncomfortable sleep but better than walking all night.

360⁰
<u>*Three Hundred and Sixty Degrees.*</u>

I was never alarm clock dependent. I have always awakened at sunrise. I turned on the washing machine and used hot water to wash up. I quietly gathered my things and crept out of the laundry room. I caught the earliest bus destined for downtown. It was Thursday, one day before payday. I was officially homeless. I needed somewhere to go until I could find a place.

I got off the bus at Ponce and fifth and went to a women's shelter for help. Addicts are very resourceful. You hear so many stories in the crack house. It seems that homelessness is part of every addict's reality at some point during the cycle of addiction.

The building had a gloomy, doomed look. It was a pretty, historic, antebellum home, but it had a gloomy aura. Hopelessness and despair permeated the atmosphere. It may have been the aura of desperation and depravity that covered the faces of the women in the long line requesting services. It may have been the look on the young children's faces as they stood in line holding tight to hands that had nothing to hold on to. I don't know what it was, but the pretty building surrounded by a nicely landscaped lawn looked doomed. The shelter didn't have an available bed for a single woman. But the counselor advised me to call back after 12:00. I really didn't want to bother calling back. As many homeless people as there are in this city, I doubt if they would ever have an opening. They are trained to leave you hopeful.

I boarded the next bus and went to work. I didn't want Cersi to know I was homeless, so I hid my things behind the file cabinet out of her view. I went about work as usual. I didn't have money to eat, so I ate some of the crackers in a basket Cersi keeps on top of a small, dorm size, refrigerator on the side of her desk. I called the women's shelter at noon. I knew it would be useless, but I called anyway. They didn't have an available bed but gave me a list of referrals. It's just like I said, they don't like leaving the homeless hopeless.

I called Andreas. He didn't answer the phone, so I paged him. I didn't want to be in a situation and not have a place to go for the night.

"Did anyone page Andreas from this number?" I was happy he responded to my page, but he was so formal; I was almost afraid to talk to him.

"Yes, it's Thandisha; I need a favor. Grandma put me out of the house."

"Why did she do that?" I could tell he was going to be judgmental, but it was no time to have pride.

"She didn't believe I was with you and Kyia."

"Why wouldn't she believe you? You must have done something to make her not trust you."

"No shit I have done a lot for her not to trust me, but not lately and definitely not yesterday. Remember I was with you and Kyia."

"I know your grandmother would not put you..." I hung up the phone. I couldn't take anymore. I didn't know where I was going after work, but I wasn't going to a dope trap, nor was I going to live on the street. I had come too far.

Khalid was the only other person I could call. I was nervous as hell dialing Grandma's phone number. I prayed Khalid would answer the phone.

"Hello," God does answer prayer and sometimes the answer is yes.

"Khalid, I am so happy to hear your voice! I know you may not believe me either, but I have not been using drugs. Last night, I was out with Kyia and Andreas. Grandma didn't believe me because..."

"Thandie stop. I believe you. Where are you?"

"I am at work. The problem is I don't have anywhere to go after work. I don't have money, and I won't have money until tomorrow. Can you loan me money for a hotel until tomorrow?"

"No Thandie, I won't loan you money. I will give you the money for a hotel. I'm also going to help you find a place to live." I gave him directions to the bookstore. I was relieved. I went about my workday as if all was well. The urge to use drugs crossed my mind, but it was definitely a passing thought. The day started out scary and filled with uncertainty but ended calm and filled with hope. I was happy and relieved; I actually forgot that it was 5:00.

"Thandisha, are you spending the night?"

"Oh no Cersi, I am finishing up some work." I didn't want her to know my situation. I was embarrassed and felt a lot of guilt. I must have been awful. Andreas knows I was with him and Kyia. For him to believe I was getting high, amazed me.

"Make sure you lock up when you leave."

"Oh sure," I was relieved when she left. I finished working on the plans for the next book signing. I couldn't very well say that I was working on a project and have nothing to show her tomorrow.

It seemed as if it were taking Khalid forever to get here. I started to panic. What if Grandma didn't allow him to leave the house? I really should not have involved him in my mess, but I was desperate. I needed to hold on to this job. It would have been almost impossible to work and not have a place to live. I am fighting hard to stay clean. I knew it wasn't going to be easy, but I didn't expect this. I expected my family to be happy for me. I didn't want a free ride just a chance. I wanted the people who professed to love me the most to believe in me, especially when I was telling the truth. I don't remember asking Grandma for anything. In fact, I stayed as far away from her, Khalid, and Aunt Mary as I could. I didn't want them to see me when I was using crack. I looked a mess. I don't care how well I attempted to dress myself up, there is something repelling about the aura of a crack addict.

I was relieved when I saw the bright lights. I wanted to get something to eat, take a hot shower and sleep on a soft, firm mattress. I was hungry; I felt as if I were at that stage where my body would soon begin digesting itself. I opened the door and waved at him, so he knew that I was still inside. I grabbed the garbage bag with my clothes from behind the file cabinet, activated the alarm, and locked the door behind me.

"Hey sis.''

"What's up?" I waved to him, as I walked to his car.

"Do you want to get something to eat first?"

"Please," fast food was exactly what I needed.

Although there were only three cars in the drive thru, it seemed as if it were taking forever to place my order. I ordered a burger and fries. I was so hungry; I practically gobbled the burger down in three bites. I looked forward to payday and having my own money. I had planned on eating at the bookstore. I had been looking at the chicken salad croissants for two weeks, but the most important thing was to secure housing. Khalid took me around the corner from my job to a residential area. I had seen a garage apartment for rent two days ago. This was not exactly what I had in mind, but I was desperate. He drove me to the apartment, so I could get the phone number before taking me to a hotel.

"Where do you want to stay?" I really had not thought about it. I simply wanted a place to lay my head.

"Pull over there Khalid." The hotel looked kind of sleazy, but I didn't care.

"Here?" He didn't like it. I didn't either; it really didn't matter because all I wanted was to watch television and take a hot bath. Khalid gave me the money to pay the room rate for one night. After I paid for the room, he got out of the car, and walked me inside of the hotel.

"Thandisha, I want you to know I believe in you. I know you are handling yourself, and I have a lot of respect for you." He reached in his pocket and pulled out three hundred and fifty dollars.

"Where did you get all of that money?"

"Look at me. Do I look like I wear the latest fashions to you?" I stared straight in his eyes waiting for an answer.

"I save my money Thandie. Where did you think I got it?"

"I don't know that's why I asked." Many of the drug dealers I used to cop from were my brother's age. I definitely didn't want my brother getting caught in the game. "Khalid, I will have to pay you back in three weeks."

"You don't have to pay me back. Just get a stable place to live and take care of yourself." Khalid left. I made myself comfortable. I called the front desk to get a wake up call so that I could get to work on time not that I needed it. I was very much in tune with the sun. I lay across the bed flipping channels. I couldn't find anything on television. I was bored, so I called Andreas to remind him that I was coming for Kyia Saturday morning.

"Hello."

"May I speak to Andreas?"

"Who is calling?" I knew it was Dee, and I knew she knew it was me. I remember feeling sorry for her when I was younger. Her sister, Ayanna, was very hard on her. I now agree with Ayanna; she is a trifling bitch.

"Could you tell him it's Thandisha?"

"Yeah." She slammed the phone down so hard it hurt my ear.

"Hello," his voice was deep and still sexy as hell.

"I was calling to remind you; I am coming for Kyia Saturday morning." He was silent.

"I'll probably be there around 9:00 am."

"I thought you said your grandmother put you out."

"She did, but we don't need to talk about that now. Do we? I will be there at 9:00." I hung up the phone and went to bed. I looked forward to tomorrow. Khalid agreed to pick me up at lunch to look for other places close to my job in case the garage apartment was no longer vacant, or for some reason the landlord wouldn't rent it to me.

As usual, the sun served as my alarm; besides, I didn't receive the wake up call I requested. I showered and listened to the morning news while getting dressed. I didn't have an iron. My clothes were slightly wrinkled, but they could pass. I stuffed my belongings in my book bag and walked to the bus stop.

Cersi was already at work when I arrived.

"Good morning."

"Good morning, Thandisha. Hey you never did get back with me about selling your art." A big smiled stretched across her entire face. "Guess what?" I didn't feel like listening, but as long as she was not telling me that I was fired, I could take any news. "Ron wants to buy that painting behind my desk."

"Are you serious?"

"Yes I am very serious. I didn't know how much you wanted for it, but I said $300.00." My eyes were probably popping out of my head.

"When does he want to pick it up?"

"He will be here after lunch and before five."

"Great!"

"You know Thandisha, this could be another avenue for the bookstore. I was thinking I could allow you to have a small space for your art behind the dining area and in return the bookstore receives thirty five percent of what you sale." This was a wonderful idea. I have several paintings in the garage at Grandma's house, plus I have a vision of a charcoal piece in my head.

Of course, Cersi typed a contract, had me sign it, and then had it notarized. And of course, the contract was retroactive. She was always about business. I would have an extra $195.00. It felt good having money again. One of the problems Andreas and I had was that I didn't save money. I decided to open an account and put money in it every payday. I hoped to never to be in this predicament again.

I went to my desk, completed the work on three book orders, and made contact with the authors' publicists. I also made contact with a Michelle Harvey, a new self-publisher. CNR was unique in that it had a section in the store for self-published writers. To my surprise, many of the self-published titles were good sellers. I really like the way some of the self-published writers conducted business, and they were much easier to work with.

At 12:00 noon, Khalid entered the bookstore just as I grabbed my jacket. Cersi met him at the door. I didn't like the way she looked at him. She smiled, throwing her sewn in hair all over the place. She was actually flirting with him.

"Hello Khalid, I see you have met Cersi, my boss." He extended his hand to her. She softly embraced his hand. I didn't like the way she smiled at him. She was behaving as if Khalid were a man instead of a boy. To my surprise, Khalid appeared to be flirting with her also.

"Come on little brother, let's go." Khalid and I left for lunch. The first thing we did was drive to the garage apartment. It was still available. I cashed my check then went back to the adjacent house and knocked on the door. A petite, middle-aged, African American woman answered the door. For some reason, I expected the owner to be white. The neighborhood used to be predominantly black; but in the last five years, most of the African Americans sold their homes to whites who wanted to return to the city. Some of the residents that didn't sale their homes lost them because their meager earnings could not keep up with the increase in property taxes due to the improvements of the new, high-income, mostly white owners. Ms. Manley introduced herself while looking at me up and down, front and center.

"How many people will be occupying the unit?"

"Mainly me, but my daughter visits me every weekend." The rent was four hundred dollars per month. I thought this was steep for a one bedroom over a garage, but I didn't have time to look for anything else. The good thing is that it was walking distance to my job, and it had hardwood floors. I gave Mrs. Manly the application fee; she instructed me to call back after two o'clock.

The rent was 400.00 with a 150.00 deposit. I would have enough to get the place, and buy a few things for the apartment. While I was out to lunch, Mrs. Manly called and left a message on my voicemail. I was happy when I found that my application was approved. I returned her call and made arrangements to bring the money, sign the lease, and get the keys. I called the utility companies and found they would bill the deposits, but the electricity would not be connected until Monday. I was still ecstatic about moving into my own place even if I did not have electricity. It would be an easy move. The only thing I had was what I carried in my garbage bag. I still had some things at Andreas'. He couldn't have thrown everything away. I knew he didn't throw away my armoire. He knew how much I loved it. It was my mother's, and he knew I cherished it.

I felt good. I was grateful. I could not have asked for a better day. I still had cravings for crack cocaine. I don't know what triggers it, but for no apparent reason, I am plagued with a reoccurring pungent odor. It starts out subtle then increases to a strong almost forceful sweet, yet pungent, odor. Thank God the obsession has been removed. I now know I don't have to use just because that smell enters my nose.

Cersi's friend, Ron, came at 3:00 to pick up the painting. He was handsome. It appeared as if Ron and Cersi were dating or at least had more than a friendly relationship because he stood fixed in her personal space, and she appeared to like it. He gave me three, pretty, one hundred dollar bills. I gave Cersi $105.00, her share of the sale. I thought thirty-five percent was really a bit much. When I factored in the time, the cost of the canvas not to mention the price for frames and matting, I really wasn't making a big profit. Ron wanted to look at more of my work. I could not tell him the other paintings are at my grandmother's home, and I am not allowed in her home. I was very embarrassed about my situation.

"I am flattered you like my work. I'll bring a couple of paintings to work on Monday." He was almost pushy about coming to look at my work. I convinced him to wait until Monday. I told him I was going to be busy all weekend. It wasn't actually a lie because I planned on cleaning my new home and finding items at the thrift stores to make it livable.

I went home after work. I paid the rent, deposit, and got the keys from Ms. Manly. The apartment reeked of mildew and musk. I didn't have the money to buy a lot of cleaning supplies. I bought bleach to disinfect and pine cleaner to give the apartment a fresh smell. I didn't have lights, so I purchased candles. I cleaned for as long as I could, as I was dependent on the sunlight from outside. After sunset, I lit the candles and read the newspaper.

I was not afraid. Although there was no electricity, I had a phone. I established phone service with a simple phone call. I sat by the candle and wrote out a list of things I needed. I didn't write down linen. I knew he didn't throw away my armoire. I kept my expensive linen in the bottom of the armoire. I had a couple of nice Egyptian cotton sheet sets that I assumed were still inside of the armoire. The crazy thing about Andreas is that although he constantly complained about my spending habits, he liked the things I purchased. I blew out the candle and went to sleep on a makeshift bed I made from a piling my clothes on top of each other.

As usual, the sun served as my alarm clock. I didn't have toothpaste or soap. I walked to McDonalds and washed up with the rough paper towels in the bathrooms. I went into one of the stalls and changed my clothes. I walked back to my apartment, put my clothes away, and caught the next bus to Andreas'. When I got off the bus, I called him from the gray, graffiti covered pay phone at the corner across the street from his apartment. He didn't answer the phone. I took my chances and walked to his apartment anyway. I told him I would be coming to visit Kyia at 9:00 a.m.

I knocked on the door; he sounded as if he were just getting out of bed.

"Who is it?"

"It's me, Thandisha." I heard a lot of movement inside of the apartment. I wasn't concerned about the female voice. I didn't come for trouble. I simply came to see my daughter.

"Hold on," he came to the door and slightly opened it; only half of his face was visible.

"What time is it?"

"It's 9:00. I told you I was coming at 9:00. I came to see Kyia. What you are doing and who you are doing it with is totally insignificant to me." He stood looking at me and then looking in the door at whoever was inside with him.

"Well come back a little later." I know this fool didn't think this was going to fly with me. He attempted to close the door. I placed my foot in the door to prevent it from closing.

"Hell no I came to see my daughter. I don't give a damn about what you have going on. In fact, you can tell Dee I said hello, but I am not leaving until I see Kyia." He turned his head and mumbled to Dee. He really was not what one could call a ladies' man. He's very good looking, but he was not one to date a lot of different women. Although I could not see inside, I knew it was Dee.

"Open the damn door Andreas, or bring my baby outside!" I was getting angry and ready to kick the damn door down if I had to. I wasn't leaving without spending time with Kyia. He didn't open the door, but I could hear a loud, shouting match between Andreas and Dee.

Initially, I was afraid when I saw the blue lights flashing and the police car speeding down the street towards me, but then I realized I was not doing anything wrong. He must have forgotten that we were not married, and there was no court order granting him custody of Kyia. That's another thing about the crack house, it's filled with street lawyers. It wasn't that I abandoned Kyia, I simply backed away because I didn't want to cause anymore harm. I did not want Kyia to see me messed up anymore.

"What is the problem ma'am?" The balding, six feet, two hundred pound, police officer had his hand on his gun approaching my small, five feet and four inch, 115 pound frame as if I were a criminal. I remained calm and kept my hands where he could easily see them.

"Sir, I really don't know. I am here to see my daughter. My ex-boyfriend has company and will not allow me to see my baby. I told him I was coming to see her at 9:00. I think he is uncomfortable because he has a woman in what used to be our home, but I am not the least upset about that. I would simply like a visit with my daughter." Andreas stood in the door with a blank look on his face.

"Sir, is there a reason she can't visit the child?"

"No, she can visit; I simply wanted her to come back later."

"Officer, he and I were never married. He has not taken me to court for custody. Can you explain to him that I can come for my child anytime because I am still her legal custodian?"

"She is right if that is the case. Do you have custody of the child?"

"Yes sir, she has always lived with me." Dee came to the door snatching it open like a wild woman.

"The reason he won't allow her to see the baby is because she is a crack head." The police officer looked shocked.

"Ma'am, are you using illegal drugs?" I had a bewildered look on my face.

"Officer, do I look like I am on drugs? I work everyday. I have my own place, and I simply came to get my daughter for a visit." Dee was ranting, raving, and cursing like a sailor. The officer threatened her with arrest before she finally calmed down. Andreas stood quiet rubbing his head in confusion.

"Andreas, all I want is a visit with Kyia." I gave him a nasty look. He appeared confused and outdone. "I told you I was coming at 9:00. If you had company or other plans, you should have come by my job or called, so we could have worked something out."

"Sir, she is right. Unless you can show legal papers stating you have custody, she can take the baby." Andreas stood speechless; actually he looked plain damn stupid.

"I don't have that. Thandisha, can you stay here with Kyia while I take Dee home? I'll come right back, and we can talk."

"That's fine with me." This gave me the opportunity to look for some of my things, and he said that he would take me shopping for clothes today. I was a winner all around.

"Is that okay with you ma'am?"

"Sure I have no problem with that." I waited outside while he and Dee dressed. I could hear Dee inside screaming at Andreas, but when they came outside, she was smiling and acting like the confident girlfriend.

"I will be back in twenty minutes."

"Sure, where are her clothes? I'll get her dressed while you are gone."

"They're in her room. I'll be right back."

"Okay, ya'll drive safe." I waved them off smiling from ear to ear.

The apartment was still nice. It was decorated the same as it was before I left. My armoire was still in the hall. The bed was covered in the same coverlet. I looked in my armoire. Thank God my coverlets and linen were still inside. I went into Kyia's room; she was still asleep. I decided not to wake her. I found her clothes, sat down, and waited for Andreas to return.

He entered the apartment speechless. It was as if he wanted to say something but did not have the verbiage to express it.

"Thandisha, I am sorry about that. I had no idea she would call the police."

"Andreas, I really don't give a damn about all of that. I told you I was coming for Kyia today. I don't know why your girlfriend got so upset."

"She's not my girlfriend."

"Well I can't tell, and we really do not have to discuss that because I really don't care. As I told you, I have too much to do to go there."

"Okay, let's not argue." He didn't want to argue. I didn't either. I would have much preferred to snatch his face off, but I focused on spending time with my daughter.

"Where did you want to go?"

"What do you mean? I came, as I told the officer, to spend time with Kyia. I have a place now, and I figured Kyia and I would go to flea markets and find a few things for my place."

"Why can't I drive you around? I really don't mind, and I would really enjoy spending time with the both of you." I hoped he didn't think I believed that. He wanted to chaperone my visit with Kyia. "Remember, I was supposed to take you shopping to buy clothes for work." I was glad he remembered.

"Well I would like some of the things you have here that belong to me like my pots and my armoire; I looked inside of it and found some of my linen."

"Okay that's fine." We sat in silence.

"So where is your place?"

"It's around the street in walking distance to my job."

"You got a place fast huh?"

"After getting put out of the house, I had to find a place fast or live on the street. I had planned on living with Grandma for six weeks, but of course, that didn't work out. She put me out."

"Thandisha, I am sorry. I guess I still have some stuff to get over." As if he was the only person who had shit to get over. Hell life has been pretty rocky for me too.

"Well that's cool believe me I didn't take it personal. After going through the hell I have been through, the only thing anyone could do to me is kill me and that's only with my God's permission."

"Well where do you want to go first?"

"First, I would like to move my armoire into my apartment. I see you didn't throw away my cookware. If you don't mind, I would like to take them with me." He looked crazy as if he couldn't believe I was asking for my things. I didn't care. I paid good money for my cookware.

He loaded my things into his truck, and we took them to my place. He even gave me the antique chair and ottoman that I picked out from the thrift store for his first apartment. He never really liked the chair anyway. My place was small and over a garage, but it was nice and cozy. The yard was well manicured with pretty flowers and green shrubbery. I was proud to call it home. There was no electricity, so the apartment was warm but still comfortable.

Andreas appeared impressed with the apartment. There is a small foyer at the entrance. The floors were walnut stained, which I preferred because it is easier to match furniture. The small amount of furniture I had made the place look nice. I put the armoire in my bedroom. I placed the chair in the living room. I had a couple of pictures in Grandma's garage I wanted to put in the living room. Of course, I couldn't go to the house. My apartment may not have been much to anyone else, but it meant a lot to me. This is the first time I have felt at home since That Day, the day my daddy killed my mother.

After placing the furniture in my apartment, we went to the mall where I enjoyed spending Andreas' money. He picked out a straight black dress that subtly fit my body. The dress came just above my ankles, and it was classy as hell. He bought a pair of up to date, high-heeled black shoes to match. I picked out two pair of dress slacks with matching tops. The clothes were basic colors, so I could mix and match them. I still do not understand why he threw my clothes away.

"I see you still have expensive taste."

"Yes I do when I am spending your money." He laughed. We were actually having a good time. Even Kyia was comfortable with me. She even called me momma. After we left the mall, we went to the thrift store. Andreas didn't want to go, but I needed a bed.

"I can't believe you are going to buy a used mattress." He turned up his nose. Initially, I thought about forgetting the mattress because he made me feel cheap. Then I thought, if he wanted me to have a better mattress, he could buy me one. As long as it is clean, there is nothing wrong with a used mattress. I wanted a bed to sleep on. Besides, Mr. Smart Ass obviously hasn't heard that bleach kills germs.

"You can tie the mattress and box spring onto the top of the truck." He looked as if he didn't want it on is new SUV, but I really didn't care. I knew his vehicle was new, but a mattress and boxspring would not hurt it. The salesclerk appeared confused as if he didn't know if he should place the mattress and box spring on top of the SUV or leave them in the store.

"Okay put them on, but carefully." Kyia and I continued to pick up a few items at the thrift store. I still had over 200 dollars. I found a small radio for three dollars and a used colored television for 50 dollars. It didn't have a remote, but that didn't matter. I could change the channels manually.

We left the thrift store and went back to my apartment again to put the bed and the other items I purchased inside. "Thandisha, since you don't have utilities you can come home with me and Kyia." I looked at him like he was crazy.

"What about Dee? What is your girlfriend going to think about that?" He was uncomfortable talking about Dee.

"She is not my girlfriend. She is a nice girl, but I don't have a girlfriend." I started to curse him out; I didn't think the bitch was nice at all.

"Well she obviously thinks she is your girlfriend. I mean she called the police on me for trying to see my own child."

"I am sorry about that. I really didn't mean for that to happen." He appeared sincere. "Come on girl, let's go. You don't need to stay here without electricity." He was right.

Besides if I went home with him, I could spend time with Kyia. I packed a bag for the weekend and included work clothes for Monday morning.

When we arrived at his apartment, the first thing he did was go to the phone and turn off the ringer. I put my things down in Kyia's room. He ordered pizza. I was glad because I was too tired to cook, and I would have felt uncomfortable cooking at his apartment; this was now another woman's kitchen.

"Momma!" Kyia yelled for me pointing at the refrigerator.

"Now what do you want in there?" It made me happy when she called me momma. I picked her up and carried her to the refrigerator. She pointed to the milk carton. I gave her a cup of milk, then took her to the bathroom, and undressed her for her bath. I ran the bath water while she played with the cabinets.

"Bubbles," her speech was not as developed as Khalid's when he was her age. She used one-word sentences and her finger to point to what she wanted. I poured bubble bath in the water and placed her in the tub. There were bubbles in her hair and all over her face. Kyia had a beautiful head of kinky, thick, jet black, hair. Her hair was long and thick like mine and momma's. Andreas really did his best to manage it, but she really needed a woman's touch. After bathing her, I allowed her to play in the water and then dried her off and put on her pajamas. I sat on the sofa and placed her between my knees and parted her hair in small sections and applied oil to her scalp. I didn't place the rubber band back in her hair. Instead, I plaited her hair and placed barrettes at the ends to keep the plaits from unraveling, the way momma used to comb my hair.

I showered after putting Kyia to bed. When I came out of the bathroom, Andreas was sitting on the sofa. I could feel his stare. I decided not to look back. I put on a t-shirt and jeans before going back in the living room.

"You know you still look nice. Was I really that bad? Did you have to leave like that?" He knew as well as I did that it wasn't him. He knows I was the problem. I was beginning to think he enjoyed hearing me put myself down.

"Andreas, you know I was on drugs. It's like your girlfriend said: I was a crack head. I couldn't enjoy you. You are a good man. I think you know that." He reached over and tried to kiss me. I pushed him away. I knew he was involved with someone. Even though I still loved him, I was not playing second fiddle. Besides, I wasn't emotionally ready for a relationship with anyone.

"I don't think this is a good idea. I think we should keep this on a friendly level and parent our child." I could tell by the bulge forming in his boxers that he didn't agree. I did us both a favor and went to Kyia's room, climbed in bed with her, and went to sleep.

I was awakened by a hard knock on the door. It sounded as if someone was trying to beat the door down. Andreas was still asleep. I went into his room to awaken him. I forgot my robe. I walked back to Kyia's room to get it. By the time I reached his door again, he was awake. He appeared reluctant to answer the door, but whoever was at the door was persistent. I went to the bathroom and showered while he answered the door. The bathroom door was closed, but I could hear every word said.

"Why didn't you answer your phone last night?"

"I was busy."

"Doing fucking what?"

"Look my daughter is in the bed, so watch your language."

"Well who the hell is in the shower?" I knew he was thinking he should have kept his mouth shut, but Andreas has always been an honest guy.

"Dee, I don't have to explain my life to you. We agreed that we are just friends. We are not committed, but if you have to know, Thandisha is spending the weekend here until her electricity is turned on Monday."

"And your ass is worried about my language, but you are not worried about a crack head around your daughter?"

"Dee, I think you better leave."

"I ain't going no damn where!" I heard him slam the door hard. I finished my shower. I dried my body as slowly as I could. I was getting tired of people referring to me as a crack head. I know for assuredly that I hurt myself more than I could have ever hurt anyone else. Thank God I was getting clean for me. I am so thankful; I no longer needed anyone's approval.

I came out of the shower with only my robe. Our eyes met. His eyes appeared remorseful. I was blank and expressionless.

"I am sorry about that."

"You know Andreas. I will be glad when everyone gets over my past because I have. I really don't care what Dee says about me. After all I've been through, I am too grateful to be alive to care about you or anyone else that sums me up in two words, crack head." I didn't give him time to say anything. I went into Kyia's room and put on my clothes. I went in the kitchen and began to make breakfast when I heard a harsh knock on the door again.

"Hello Dee, how are you?" She didn't say anything. I wanted to give her the opportunity to talk to the crack head face to face. "It's as Andreas said. I am here spending the weekend until Monday morning when my utilities are turned on. You called the police on me because I was trying to visit my child. You referred to me as a crack head in hearing range of my baby. I am not going to waste my time attempting to convince you that I am not a crack head. You are too insignificant to my life, but I will tell you this." I paused while I looked at her up and down. "You can say anything you want to say about me. Who cares? But you will not disrespect me in the presence of my child.

Remember I am still her mother, and I don't care how much or
how good you fuck Andreas. That will never change." I looked
at her; she looked at me. I opened the door as wide as it would
go and yelled as loud as I could, "Andreas, you have a guest!"

He came to the door. I left the living room. He didn't
invite her inside. Instead, they went outside. He was outside for
several minutes before coming back inside. He didn't say
anything and neither did I.

We sat down, ate breakfast and watched television. I knew
he was embarrassed. Regardless of what I've done, he knows
me. He has a great deal of information on me, as I have a great
deal of information on him. I knew he still loved me. There are
some loves that just don't go away. I am not saying I am so
great, but he remembers. He remembers when I was innocent.
Don't get me wrong. He knows the other side of me too.

I know that no matter how he tries he can't sum me up as a
crack head; he knows there is much more to me than that. The
active addiction was not my life. It was a moment in my life. He
knew me before I became an active addict. He knows the trauma
I experienced when my father killed my mother. Andreas
understands my pain, and he knows the progress I have made.
He may have a sexual relationship with another woman, but he
will always love me. My only advice to Dee is that she not get
attached.

I would have made a Sunday dinner but decided I would
cook for Kyia when she visits. I do not want Andreas to think I
am trying to come back into his life at this point. I want to grow
and get to know myself, so I can get the strength to truly face my
trauma. I am determined; it will no longer hold me hostage.
Whatever happens, I will be okay.

Monday morning came fast. I enjoyed my weekend stay
with Andreas and Kyia. It was fun; I had the opportunity to
spend time with my daughter with a clear mind, but I was glad to
go to my own home. I looked forward to cleaning my home and

organizing it. Granted I wasn't working with much, but having my own roof was a great feeling.

Andreas gave me a ride to work. Cersi was already at her desk working when I arrived. She was dry, but I have learned not to allow other people's mood swings determine the outcome of my day. I worked on the itinerary for the next book-signing event. I made sure that all of my "T's" were crossed and "I's" dotted. I was already under close scrutiny from every one else in my life, so I could handle anything Cersi threw at me.

"Thandisha, I thought you finished your next book event already." I didn't know where she was going, but I figured she was indirectly asking me what I was working on.

"Yes, I did. I am working on the next event."

"Well what event is that?" I smiled to conceal the fact that she was getting on my nerves.

"Well you know Ashley Griffith changed plans. She wants her personal trainer and her cook to accompany her. I reserved separate suites on different floors, but she insists they all have rooms on the same floor preferable with adjoining rooms. I could not find a hotel to meet her accommodations." I was smiling on the outside but on the inside I really wanted to tell her that she could organize the event her damn self if she did not trust my judgment.

"Where is she staying?"

"She now wants to stay in a Bed and Breakfast. She is willing to pay all of the expenses. She wants it to herself for the weekend, so it's a matter of booking a weekend that it is totally empty."

"She can't do that. That's way too expensive." She walked over and looked at my outline then stood over me looking at Ashley Griffith's file. I thought to myself, *Who is she to say what someone does with their own money?* Besides, Ashley is not paying for this herself. She gave me a credit card that she says belongs to a gentleman that she describes as a very good friend to pay for the expenses.   The account was verified, so what's the problem?

"Well she obviously thinks she can afford it. I think she is going to stay for a few days. She is always asking questions about the city. I get the impression she may relocate here." I smiled in a futile attempt to create a more harmonious atmosphere.

"Relocation services are not something we offer."

"Okay, I thought that if I were accommodating, then it would be a plus for CNR's impeccable reputation."

"Well let me do all of the thinking here okay." I managed to produce a smile.

"Sure Cersi, you're the boss." She returned an equally insalubrious smile. Cersi was beginning to get on my nerves. Her mood swings were without provocation and usually caught me off guard. I wanted to work long enough to save a little money. It was important that I keep this job. Not only because I have rent to pay, but the job was good for my self-esteem. Besides, in a few months, I could get the money momma left me and maybe start my own business. I continued to work. I decided not to have lunch; instead, I looked at business start up books in the bookstore. If I could organize the events at CNR, then I could put something together for myself. I knew I had the talent, but I needed to polish my business skills.

One thing for sure, Cersi really had her stuff together. The bookstore was nice. It had a very classy atmosphere. It's in an ideal location. She has managed to grab and hold on to a loyal clientele.   Regardless of her personality, I was grateful she hired me. After working for CNR for this short time, I have learned the ins and outs of operating a business. I often sit and watch her negotiate with vendors. I took notes and started planning for my own art gallery and dessert shop.   Initially, I would not have a lot of overhead because I could do all of the cooking and then train someone else to do it for me as my business grows.

"Hi," I was sitting on a ladder in the business section reading when he walked over to me. I had seen him in the bookstore several times.

"Hello," I hoped he was not going to ask for assistance. I was at lunch, and I really didn't want to be disturbed.

"Do you need help? There's a clerk at the front. I am on break."

"No, I've been in here everyday for the last month building up the nerve to approach you. Do you mind if I sit down?"

"Help yourself," I gave him a quick, pretentious smile and continued to read my book.

"You know today is my lucky day."

"Good," it had to be obvious that I was annoyed.

"My name is Elliot." He extended his hand. I lightly touched his hand in a soft, half handshake, embrace that Grandma describes as a feminine handshake where you give a man four of your fingers and lightly touch the inside of his hand.

"So what are you reading?"

"How to books."

"How to what?"

"How to start your own business. I'm thinking about opening up my own art gallery and dessert shop."

"Really?" He sounded interested.

"Yes."

"So you like art?"

"Yes. I'm an artist. Did you see the pictures at the front entrance? That's some of my work."

"There is a lot of money in that. I work at a brokerage house, so I know where the money is." I assumed that I was supposed to be impressed, but I wasn't.

"Oh that's nice." I gave him a fake smile and quickly placed my head back in my book.

"Do you go out much?"

"No, I don't."

"I'd like to take you out. What are you doing on Saturday?"

"My daughter usually visits on the weekends, so I do baby stuff."

"All weekend?"

"Yes all weekend from Friday night until Sunday night."

"Well what are you doing tonight? Do you like jazz? You know there is a concert in the park." Andreas is the only man I have dated. While I was using drugs, I didn't date men. A lot of women resort to trading sex for drugs, but I am thankful to God that it didn't take me there. I am sure that if I had continued, I would have started trading sex for drugs. The drug is so powerful that you loose all morals and values for one hit. I didn't have to because I stole money from Andreas to support my habit.

The idea of getting dressed up began to excite to me. I agreed to go with him to the jazz concert. I didn't have anyone to share in the excitement. Ayanna was the only friend I had since momma was killed, and we went our separate ways after I became pregnant with Kyia. Honestly, she dumped me. I should have known that the pregnancy would end our friendship because Ayannna was very focused. She stays on her path and does not allow deviations or distractions in her life.

I didn't give him my number. I took his instead. The experiences I had while using drugs made me somewhat untrusting of people. I was not ready for visitors. I enjoyed my space at home, and I really looked forward to my peace and solitude. Besides, the only reason I had a phone was for Kyia, otherwise; I would not even have one.

"I will call you, and we can set up a time to meet."

"Cool, one thing, are you going to tell me your name?"

"Thandisha," I was embarrassed; I didn't want my lack of experience in the dating game to be so obvious.

"Thandisha," I looked towards the front of the store. It was Monnighan, one of the front desk clerks at the bookstore. She initiates conversation with me sometimes. I actually enjoy talking to her. We are about the same age. She is a student at one of the historically black colleges in Atlanta. She motioned for me to come to the counter.

"Hey girl, how is it going?" She was smiling as usual.

"Pretty good, I have been working my butt off on this last book signing."

"Really, who is coming next?"

"Ashley Griffith."

"Who?" She covered her mouth in disbelief. "Oh no she didn't! Thandisha, do you know who Ashley Griffith is?" She didn't give me time to answer. "Ashley used to work here. She stole Cersi's husband." It all made sense now. Cersi has been a bitch since I booked Ashley. I knew she was divorced, but I had no idea another woman was involved. I don't understand why she allowed me to book Ashley. I didn't understand why Ashley would even want an event in Cersi's bookstore.

I felt good for the rest of the day. I hated that Cersi would have to endure whatever emotion Ashley's book signing stirred within her, but I was relieved to know that I was not the problem. I was also super excited because I had a date. I was on a natural high. My natural endorphins were working again. It's truly amazing how crack numbs you. It cuts off all you your emotions where you cannot feel. I didn't need any unnatural product in my body to make me happy or high. I was on a cloud and floating twenty-four-seven.

The apartment was cool; thank God for electricity. It was nice and cozy. I set the alarm on my radio to come on at 5:15 p.m., so I entered my apartment to the sound of cool jazz. I went to the kitchen, lit coconut incense, and poured a glass of fruit punch; I no longer drank alcohol. I was too afraid that it would trigger my addiction.

I showered, put on my black slacks, and a very sheer black shirt with a black blazer. Grandma used to say that I should wear more pastel colors. She used to complain that I always looked as if I were in mourning. I don't know if I was still mourning, but I knew I looked sexy as hell. I was still very natural. The only makeup I wore was lipstick, and I still wore my hair in the bun pulled back from my face. I probably needed to update my hair, but I still looked good, damn good in fact.

I heard someone coming up the stairs and then I heard that beautiful whiny voice. I opened the door before they knocked. Andreas was standing at the door with Kyia in his arms.

"Momma," she leaped from his arms to mine. She always feels so good. Although she was sweaty and smelled like a wet puppy, she smelled good to me.

"Hey baby. What brings you guys over here?"

"Momma," she smiled while continuously jumping up and down in my arms.

"We were in the neighborhood, and Kyia wanted to see you."

"You are so sweet. You wanted to see your momma."
She smiled and clung to me with her arms around my shoulders and her legs tightly locked around my waist.

"You look nice."

"Thanks. Do you want something to drink? I have fruit punch."

"No, I have to go. I need to put Kyia to bed."

"No daddy," she whined and pouted.

"Girl, it's almost 9:00. You are one hour past your bedtime." He sat on the chair and his eyes were fixated on me.

"So how is it going?"

"Everything is okay."

"I see you're painting again." He walked by the window and looked at my canvas then glanced at my desk. He was still so damn nosey. He walked back over to the window and looked at the canvas again.

"Wanna stay with momma."

"Oh baby, not tonight. Momma is going out tonight. Maybe daddy will let you spend the night tomorrow night."
He looked puzzled.

"Who is the lucky guy?"

"Just a guy I met at the bookstore. We're going to listen to live jazz."

"Do you think you are ready to have a relationship so soon?"

"Actually it's not a relationship. It's a date."

"Same thing."

"It's not the same thing."

"Well I don't want any man you meet in the street around my daughter."

"Do you really have control over that?" I would usually get angry when he was so controlling but not today.

"Yes, I think I do. I can control who is around my daughter and ain't no street thug coming around my daughter." He was pushing it. I changed, but I was now wise enough to know people, including my baby's daddy, would still use my past against me at their convenience.

"Actually, he is not a street thug."

"Yeah right." Initially, I was going to meet Elliot at the train station but after Andreas' sarcasm, I decided to allow him to pick me up at my apartment. I went in the bedroom, called Elliot, and gave him directions. I was putting earrings in my ear when I walked back into the living room. He was still sitting looking at the wall probably trying to think of something stupid to say.

"I don't have control of you, but I do have control of what happens to my daughter."

"Yeah I know. I guess that's why I found my best friend's sister naked in my bed with my man who was also butt naked, and the baby was in the house. I guess that was such a high class thing to do."

"I apologized for that. Remember?"

"Yes I do, and until now, I don't think I ever threw that in your face. Did I?"

Elliot's strong, confidant knock startled Andreas.

"Oh that must be him. Kyia give momma some sugar. I'll call you tomorrow; maybe daddy will let you spend the night tomorrow." I opened the door. Elliot looked surprised to find Andreas and Kyia sitting comfortably in my apartment. I introduced them, and we left. Kyia was in my arms. Andreas followed behind us. I gave Kyia to her father then walked over to the passenger side of the black Mercedes convertible where Elliot stood waiting with the door open for me. I didn't look back at Andreas, but I could feel his stare.

"Do you and your baby's father still see each other?"

"No, but we are still very cordial. We stay cordial for Kyia. We are still raising our daughter together. She stays with him during the week, and I get her from Friday until Sunday. He is more financially able to care for her right now, so this is good for all concerned. Plus he is a very good father."

"It's Wednesday."

"Yeah I know." I didn't feel the need to explain. This was just a date, and I didn't owe him an explanation.

Cars never really impressed me. To think of it nothing material impressed me. When I think back, I have always had most of the material things that I wanted. But it felt good riding in his car. It was a smooth ride and very comfortable inside. We drove to the park with the top down.

The music was nice. We ate wings; he drank a Stoley tonic, and I drank cola over ice. We ate and danced. I truly had a nice time. Elliot had good conservation. He dates a lot. He says that he has never found the right woman to settle down with.

"I have never really dated; actually, my daughter's father is the only guy I have ever dated."

"He's a lucky man." Actually we both were lucky. Although our relationship has been strained, I still have a great deal of respect for Andreas. We danced until 1:00 am; I wasn't tired, but I still had two more days until the weekend. I had to have the energy to work and care for Kyia from Friday until Sunday.

The ride back to my apartment was quiet and relaxing. He walked me to the door and kissed me on my cheek before leaving.

"I'd love to see you again."

"We'll see." I thanked him for a nice time and locked the door. I showered, put on my nightgown, and was ready to get in bed when I heard a strong, quick knock on the door.

"Who is it?"

"It's me." I opened the door cracking it a little. He squeezed his way in.

"Is there something wrong with Kyia?"

"No, she is fine. She spent the night with momma."

"Well what are you doing here? It's late." He didn't say anything. He sat down on the chair.

"Are you going to see him again?"

"Yeah I think so. I had a nice time."

"Don't you think it's too soon to start dating? I mean you do know that it's not over between us. Don't you?"

"I know. It will never be over. We have a daughter that we both love. We still have elementary school, high school, and college for Kyia to work out. Hell one day we will even be grandparents." I laughed, but he was still very serious.

"I don't want you to see him again Thandisha."

"Well I probably will see him again because I had a good time."

"What in the hell does that mean?"

"Andreas, I was gone less than two weeks before Dee was in my bed."

"Thandisha, you know that it didn't mean anything. Besides, you left. I didn't put you out. You left to be with your crack head friends. Can you imagine the hurt and pain I felt when I found out my favorite girl in the world was on crack? Can you imagine my fear when you would just leave in the middle of the night, and I wouldn't see you for hours hell even days?" He placed his head in his hands and stared at the floor.

"Thandisha, you put me through hell."

"I believe you, but I've been through a lot of pain, and my main focus is to heal myself and become a whole person."

"I can see; Thandisha, you are doing a good job." He came over to me, reached out for me, and pulled me close in his arms.

"You are looking really good baby." He placed a soft, moist kiss in the middle of my forehead. I felt a pleasant, tingling sensation between my thighs. It had been a while since I made love to Andreas. He was always so sensuous and gentle. My body craved him right now.

"Who do you belong too?"

"Myself," I kissed him back. I managed to tell him that I had to go to bed between kisses, but he acted as if he didn't hear me. He put his hands inside of my panties. It always felt good when he touched me there.

"I think you should go Andreas." I pulled him closer to me.

"Don't worry baby I have no expectations. I have no demands. I just want to love you right here and right now." He picked me up and carried me into my bedroom.

"Does it still feel good to you baby?" I didn't say a word. I let my body do all of the talking.

0^0
<u>Zero Degrees</u>

I loved Andreas, but I enjoyed my own space. I loved my freedom. I could finally be myself without the stress of living up to others' expectations. When I lived with Grandma, I was expected to grieve the way she wanted me to grieve which really meant that I was simply supposed to bury my pain deep inside of me, and act as if the day my father killed my mother never happened. I was unable to live up to Grandma's expectations. I always did something to piss her off. I was not outgoing, a trait she loved in my ex-best friend, Ayanna. I used to get jealous at the way she easily smiled with Ayanna and how easy it was for them to talk to one another. I believe that her main issue with me was my genetic make up. I was my mother's daughter and my daddy's girl. I think we would have gotten along better if she could have erased my paternal DNA. Maybe when she looked into my eyes, she saw daddy's eyes, and maybe that was too painful. Maybe we were all mentally ill because we never dealt with my mother's death. I don't blame her. I am not angry with her. I truly believe that she did her best. I simply wished that she could have accepted me for who I am and provided the environment for me to grieve my mother's death and my father's imprisonment.

It was 5:15. I was still working because CNR was expecting a large crowd for the Ashley Griffith book signing. I sent invitations to all of the librarians, language art teachers and college professors as well as a mass email invite to the clientele on our VIP list. Her book was number one on the best seller's list, and she recently sold her movie rights to an award-winning producer. After I placed posters at the book-signing site, I came back to the office. Cersi was sitting at her desk with her head face down on the desk. Initially, I thought she was asleep. When she raised her head off of the desk, it was obvious that she was crying. Her eyes were red and her nostrils were covered with faint traces of dried mucous. I wanted to turn around and leave the office, but our eyes met.

"Cersi, are you okay?" I walked close to her desk and gently placed my hand on her shoulder. She immediately stood and grabbed me clinging to me as if her life depended on some supernatural force that I could transcend to her. I stood motionless. I was shocked. I could never have imagined Cersi in this state. I imagined her strong and impenetrable.

"Oh God, Thandie how could he do this? How could he leave me for that trifling bitch? She was my fucking friend." Between tears and screams, I learned that the "he" was her ex-husband, and the "trifling bitch" was Ashley Griffith. It took a while for her to get herself together. She talked between sobs, but I could not understand anything she said.

"Cersi, if this bothers you so much, then why did you allow her to promote her book here?"

"I will not give those bastards the satisfaction of knowing they could get next to me." She reached into her desk and pulled out a brown, half pint bottle. She untwisted the top and took a long, hard gulp.

"Cersi, you don't have to prove anything to anyone. If this bothers you, then cancel her signing." She quickly stood and wiped the alcoholic residue from the top of her lip.

"Never, I will get through this. I will get through this."
She hugged me, grabbed her purse and left. I went to my desk,
organized my files, then locked up the store and left for the day.

I walked to the corner deli for take out. I was anxious to
get home. I created a nurturing and peaceful environment in my
home. It gave me the opportunity to finally grieve for my mother
and father. Initially, I was afraid to stay alone, but now I love it.

I stopped at the mailbox, gathered my mail, and went
inside. My apartment was still relatively bare, which is the way I
liked it. The space was therapeutic. I sat in my chair and placed
the mail on the ottoman. I opened each piece, as I gobbled down
my food. Most of the envelopes contained bills. The last letter
looked peculiar. It was course with ragged edges. There was no
return address. The enveloped looked as if it were made of
recycled paper that had been recycled over and over and over
again. I slowly opened the envelope;

My Dearest Thandie:

*It feels quite awkward writing you. Actually I do not
feel that I have the right to contact you. I understand if you
discard this letter without reading it. I would definitely deserve
that. It has been a long time Thandie. There has not been a day,
an hour, or second that you or your brother were not on my mind.
The first thing that I would like to say is I am so very sorry. I
know that my apology is almost an insult, but my limited
vocabulary does not contain the words that could explain the
regrets I have for my selfish act. I would like to say that I did
not intend to kill your mother. I loved her more than life itself. If
you can go back and try to remember some of the things that
transpired before that fatal day when I killed my beloved wife,
your beautiful mother, maybe you can see that it was truly an
accident. I had no intention of killing her. I was trying to scare
her into staying with me. I was attempting to scare her into*

loving me again. At that time in my life, I was a very scared and insecure young man. My only goal during this time in my marriage was working to take care of my family. I was determined to build an empire so that my family would not have to scrape the bottom of the barrel. In the process of living this dream, I lost my wife. When Riley, was searching for and gaining her independence, I became threatened, lost and scared. I could not imagine a life without her. She was the world to me. The night I accidentally killed her she was going to leave me. She already had an apartment and was packing her clothes to leave. I could not bare it. I initially threatened her, but she would not back down. She continued to pack her things. When I pulled the gun out and pointed it at her she still did not budge. Instead, she came towards the loaded gun. My finger was on the trigger. I was startled, and the gun went off. I make no excuses for my actions. I take full responsibility. It has taken me a while to contact you. I was too afraid.

Khalid has kept me abreast on your life. I understand that you have had an issue with substance abuse. It slipped out, so please do not be angry with your brother. He was discussing how well you are doing in your own apartment now, and he mistakenly told me of your addiction to crack cocaine. I am sorry, for I take full responsibility for that. I do not want to bombard you, nor do I want to take too much of your time. I will not write you again until I hear from you. You are forever in my prayers.

I love you Thandie
Daddy

My heart began to beat rapidly. I was so emotional that it became difficult to breathe. The tears began to flow uncontrollably. I ran to the phone.

"Hello."

"Andreas...please," I could barely talk between screams."

"Thandisha, Thandisha, calm down. Are you okay? What's wrong? Baby slow down and talk to me." I could not say anything. I was a ball of emotion. "Thandisha, I am on my way."

I sat absorbed in my pain, feeling every emotion. I longed to see him to touch him to slap him maybe even shoot him too. I was happy to read words from daddy. I was angry with him. I loved him. I hated him. I felt so many emotions simultaneously. Initially, I didn't hear the knock at the door.

"Thandisha, open the door! Open the door baby!" I somehow pulled myself off of the floor and made it to the door. I collapsed in his arms at the threshold. He carried me to the chair.

"Baby what the hell is wrong?" I couldn't say anything. I simply gave him the letter. He read the letter silently to himself. When he finished reading the letter, he placed it down on the floor. He pulled me out of the chair, and held me. I still could not speak. I didn't have words. I could see the beginning of tears forming in his eyes. He was speechless. I didn't need to hear words. I wanted to finally feel all of these emotions. I cried so hard and so long until I fell asleep. It was a long, relaxing, and peaceful sleep…

The door made a loud noise, as she walked back and forth, in and out, of the house each time carrying a bag of her things. I wondered where Khalid and I were going to sit in the car. She placed her things in the front and back seats of the new Volvo Station Wagon daddy bought her a month ago. Daddy continued to beg her to stay.

"Jikki, I am tired of your shit. I told you when I finished my GED that I was going to school. I told you when I finished the certificate program that I was going to get a job."

"Riley, what about my fucking kids? Who is going to take care of them? You don't have to work. You don't need to work. I have enough rental property so that you don't have to work. I have a successful business. Why do you think I worked so hard all of these years?"

"So you can maintain all of the damn control!" She walked close to him and screamed in his face.

"Baby, you can work for me."

"Are you fucking deaf? I don't want to work for you. I don't want this damn house. I want me. I want to get to know me. I have been with you since I was fucking 14 years old. If it weren't for the abortions I've had, I would have stayed barefoot and pregnant.

"What fucking abortion? When did you have an abortion?" He gritted his teeth so hard that his bottom jawbone protruded from his face.

"Oh baby not an abortion try three or four." She sounded as if she were enjoying her performance. She acted as if she had been harboring feelings for years and now rejoicing with an almost violent release. She laughed as if she were enjoying this power over daddy.

"You fucking bitch, how could you..." I immediately heard three loud slaps alternating with screams from momma.

"Go on hit me Jikki. It doesn't matter now. It's over. The door opened then abruptly closed again. Momma and daddy were screaming at one another again. Khalid ran into his room. I sat quietly in the den and hoped that they would stop fighting. Praying that she would give in, they would go in their room, and close the door and daddy would make her make those weird sounds, but she didn't.

Instead, I heard a loud, hollow popping followed by an eerie, echoing silence. I slowly walked into my parents' room. Momma was a folded heap in daddy's arms; blood oozed...